A PLACE CALLED ANTELOPE

The Rajneesh Story

Donna Quick

A PLACE CALLED ANTELOPE—The Rajneesh Story

First Edition limited to 1,000 copies

Published by:
August Press
Post Office Box 337
Ryderwood, Washington 98581

Library of Congress Catalog Card Number: 94-79020

ISBN: 0-9643118-0-1

Printed by Gorham Printing, Rochester, Washington

This story is loving dedicated
to the other
thirty-nine residents
of Antelope, Oregon
who were my neighbors.

Acknowledgments

To my high school classmate, mentor and friend, Professor Roy Paul Nelson of the University of Oregon, for whom I have the utmost respect, I give my heartfelt gratitude in return for his unfailing encouragement, support and enthusiasm in the writing and publishing of *A Place Called Antelope*.

To my Antelope neighbor, Frances Dickson, I give my thanks for providing the history of the Antelope church.

I thank Robert W. Chandler of the *Bend Bulletin* and Dan Spatz of The Dalles *Weekly Reminder* for graciously granting me permission to photocopy from their newspapers.

*This story is loving dedicated
to the other
thirty-nine residents
of Antelope, Oregon
who were my neighbors.*

Acknowledgments

To my high school classmate, mentor and friend, Professor Roy Paul Nelson of the University of Oregon, for whom I have the utmost respect, I give my heartfelt gratitude in return for his unfailing encouragement, support and enthusiasm in the writing and publishing of *A Place Called Antelope.*

To my Antelope neighbor, Frances Dickson, I give my thanks for providing the history of the Antelope church.

I thank Robert W. Chandler of the *Bend Bulletin* and Dan Spatz of The Dalles *Weekly Reminder* for graciously granting me permission to photocopy from their newspapers.

Preface

Our society is festering with a cankerous disease whose victims are robbed of their inherent ability to function through self-determinations.

Destructive cults are growing in number, entrapping people of all ages, creeds, races and backgrounds. Intelligence is not a bulwark against a skillful recruiter who may wear red, bib overalls or, most likely, a three-piece suit. Those who would follow a cult leader are often systematically subjected to mind control sessions which replace self-will with robotic compliance.

This story of the Rajneesh cult could have been published several years ago; however, it encompasses such unbelievable events and improbable encounters that it was prudent to set it aside until the maneuvers of cults were better known, and now cults are often in the news, and so it is time to expose, to all who will read, a deadly force which destroys human minds in order to satisfy a megalomaniacal dream.

"Once it would have shocked me to think that I could become so involved in something that I no longer cared about understanding what was going on, that I lost all critical faculties. I don't know if I'm a victim of hypnotism, or am deluded, if I've killed all trace of intelligence and am reduced to a state of idiocy, or if this is what trust is, (or) if this is no-mindfulness. It doesn't matter anymore—for better or worse, I am a goner!" (the Diary of Ma Deve Weechee, *The Further Shore*, pg. 36)

"After you turn everything over to Bhagwan, you become sort of hospitalized. You are never denied your freedom to leave, but after an extended stay it is all but impossible to face the reality of life outside." (*Life* Magazine, Nov. 1981, Iha Sayd, pg. 30)

Every word in this revealing, firsthand account is true. Every event is factual. Names have not been changed or omitted in order to protect anyone.

.

ONE

Only two kinds of people visit Antelope, Oregon: those who are there deliberately and those who are lost. This is because Antelope's Main Street is not a direct route to anyplace. I was in this Oregon Hinterland, one hundred fifty miles from Portland, searching for antique quilts and Oriental rugs.

Micky Lou Snodgrass, proprietor of the Riverside Hotel in Maupin, suggested I take the Bakeoven Road at the Deschutes River Bridge, as it would lead to the ghost town of Shaniko. Antelope, she said, was eight miles downhill from there.

It was 1970, the end of May, and the grasses of the high desert country appeared parched. The land looked worthless to my untrained city eyes. Huge outcroppings of rocks formed ridges and gullies which crossed and recrossed. Small alfalfa and wheat field serpentined narrowly through the crooked ravines as if an artist had taken the liberty of painting these brilliant crop colors were a river should flow.

The secondary road from Shaniko to Antelope was a kaleidoscope of scenery, changing from flat grassland with far-off horizons to steep hairpin turns winding downhill on a road built by nature's creatures centuries ago.

Suddenly ahead of me in the distant draw, framed by the canyon walls, I saw a small patch of green. Tall trees scattered throughout broke the skyline and gave the green blotch a ragged look, but once on Main Street I found a ticky-tacky tidy town that qualified for the Good Housekeeping Seal of Approval.

On the right, century-old poplars lined the street shading the fenced and clipped lawns which accented the small Victorian cottages, some white, grey, green, yellow, brown and one pink. Each house boasted its own distinctive gingerbread trim.

On the left side of the road stood an obtrusive two story building with the flat roof typically found in dry country. An

American flag waved over its schoolyard, and beyond the school was infinity. In only a minute of observation, the eyes could scan hundreds of acres of grazing and farm land broken only by the distant hills where they disappeared into the sky.

In the Antelope store and eight-stool cafe, I found faces that questioned my appearance in their town. Small-town folks have a knack for detecting a stranger as soon as he enters town and just as quickly making him feel welcome before he leaves. I visited with Antelopeans Doris, Mona, and Al using the key that always opens the door to friendly exchange—a smile. After buying a guilt top from Betty across the street form that one and only business enterprise, I drove through Pine Canyon to Fossil where Jessie Faye Morris was conducting a garage sale. How opportune for me! Not only did I buy some antiques from her, but I made an acquaintance which provided good reason to travel this same picturesque route many times in the years to come.

The spirit of adventure overtook me that May as I left my seven-acre miniranch on the outskirts of Portland where I spent most of the summer's time dragging a three gallon spray tank up and down the cow pasture killing the weeds and spent the winters locked in because I was afraid to return home after dark due to frequent burglaries in the area. I began telling my friends that I had to move to a small, crime-free community that boasted a rural atmosphere, had a grocery store in the event I was unable to drive in my old age, and most important—I required a good nearby neighbor for security purposes.

"There's a house for sale in Antelope next to our friends Tiny and Agnes." It was unbelievable! Such an outlandish coincidence that in Antelope, the oasis of the desert country, the town with a movie-set charm, a vacancy existed. I had met Enid and Lee Nichols years earlier when he repaired an old saddle for me. We visited often so we could swap tall horse tales, and elderly Lee could spin some fascinating yarns about his days as camp cook on cattle drives throughout Nevada, Idaho, and Montana. It was Enid who told me the good news,

news that would alter my life adversely with circumstances that would nearly destroy my health and surely break my heart.

It was the pink house on the corner of Main and Baird Streets that I bought with my heart. The full front porch supported with ornate white posts, the large bay window and transomed front door told me my old furniture would be happily housed therein.

Ceilings had to be raised to their original height, and the old plaster which contained horse and human hair as a binder had to be patched. I found myself nervously perspiring on the fourth and fifth rungs of the ladder as I overhauled the ten foot ceilings. Before the pink house, the second rung was the limit.

Dark paneling had to be removed from the walls in order to hang wallpaper dripping with garlands of pink roses. Picture molding was tacked in place. A functional, authentic parlor stove was placed over burgundy tile, and burgundy carpeting the same shade as the upholstery on the Eastlake rockers was installed. The melodeon looked best in the front window, and the pink sofa fit perfectly into the bay window. The parlor was then ready for company and the serving of tea and crumpets.

The dining room had its own woodstove and was separated from the kitchen by a bar which served as a back for the kitchen stove. The kitchen boasted flour and sugar bins built under a screened pie cupboard. The original kitchen cabinets had to be steam cleaned to remove layers of paint and reveal the pine and cedar woods beneath. Three applications of pure tung oil were then hand-rubbed into those old cupboard boards before the original kitchen latches, patented 1897, were attached.

Several of the doors in the house had lost their original porcelain knobs, but a search of secondhand shops in Portland provided the needed hardware. The rejuvenation of the pink house and the landscaping of its yard deprived me of nearly a year of oil painting and story writing, yet I had but one regret—I should have moved to the picturesque hamlet when I first discovered it.

Tiny and Agnes were my nearest and dearest neighbors. I knew I had chosen the right town when she told me Antelope had never had a documented crime. "There's nothing to fear here, but watch out for the rattlesnakes when you pull your rhubarb." Tiny gave her a wished-you-hadn't-said-that look. He knew I would panic at the very thought of seeing a rattlesnake—so that was why he had removed all the tall grass from the wet spot under the backyard water spigot.

I asked him one day why there wasn't a gate in the fence between our yards. We had to walk a long way to get around that fence in order to visit. It was Agnes who answered, "Tiny never wanted a gate in that fence." However, upon a return home from a trip to Portland, there it was, a dandy gate. It didn't take long to wear a path between our back doors.

Tiny didn't like dogs. He said he knew it was something psychological, but anytime he touched a dog he could smell the critter for three days. One day he rapped on my back door, and there in his arms was my own Tizzy Lish whom he had found headed down Main Street with some unknown destination in mind. Another time I was sitting with Agnes in her front room and in came Tiny with Tizzy Lish at his heels. Tizzy knew how to smile and use the "key" to friendly exchange, too.

Tiny had been a horseman all his life, and so when I brought a two-year-old colt to Antelope, he was pleased to have a saddle horse to ride, and I was delighted to have him gentle the colt. One day he rode him over to the Bob Kauer ranch, (the Antelope Ranch) to see if he'd "watch cows." He returned from the ride very satisfied with Sage. He said he had the making of a good cowhorse. An hour later he died with his boots on.

Tizzy Lish spent the day of his memorial service sitting on his back porch and would not answer my call to come home. I had to carry her away. We felt the loss of a special friend.

Agnes and I drew close. Many an enjoyable evening we spent together in her home where she would play her electronic organ, and I'd try to sing. We ate ice cream and cookies at her house, but when she visited me, we sipped creme sherry. The first time we had a drink together, I had not yet hung the parlor curtains, and we laughed as we guessed what the town gossips might say if they saw us, neither of us caring.

Gossips seem more prevalent in a small town. Antelope's residents were divided into factions, those who never spoke to each other due to a long ago feud; those who never ventured from their premises except to pick up mail or to leave town; those who had known each other previously at the Gresham Elk's Lodge, and those whose kin had pioneered in the area. Some of these latter were prone to take charge of all social and civic functions, and should one refuse to conform to orders imposed by these few old-timers who believed that Antelope was indeed "their town" that one would be ostracized—never notified of public functions, never visited and generally ignored. Sometimes blackmail was applied to bend a strong-willed dissenter.

I was resident number thirty-nine and enjoyed visitations from most of the ladies in town and from nearby ranches from time to time. I never suspected that each select group was vying for my allegiance, and regardless of the tales told by local Antelopeans about the eccentricities of their neighbors, I carefully selected those who would be welcome in my parlor.

The day of Tiny's memorial service I met Darleen Osborne as she delivered pies and dinner rolls to Agnes. We exchanged greetings. It was early summer and within one week her husband arrived at my back gate with his garden tiller to till the weeds from my garden. He knew Tiny had done many helpful deeds for me.

Darlene and I found we shared the same thoughts on many issues. Almost daily we would hike out Bennett Road toward Black Rock Ranch as we discussed city politics with much fervor.

One of the highlights of that summer was the opportunity to ride horseback in the Black Rock country. Mayor Mobley saddled two of his cowhorses and his wife and I, with ample lunch in the saddle bags, spent a delightful day visiting old homesteader's cabins (always fastening the doors shut to keep a calf from wandering in and shutting the door and thus starving to death). We visited a huge sheep shearin' shed complete with a three compartment outhouse to accommodate the herders who would gather there the day the shearers arrived. I felt particularly privileged to see this back country since only from horseback or by walking many miles was it accessible.

At the far end of the block from the pink house is the Silvertooth house where Janet Stewart and Mildred Silvertooth were born. Their father, John, was born there in 1885 and was proprietor of many of Antelope's business establishments including the famous Idle Hour Saloon. He was a pioneer of note, an entrepreneur, a champion of Antelope and a caring neighbor. His grandson would later prove to be worthy of his name, when he deliberately assumed a position between the residents of Antelope and a treacherous enemy.

The Silvertooth house, though furnished just as it was when old John was alive, was unoccupied except on those weekends when Mildred and Janet visited to enjoy the place of their childhood and also refurbish the old structure. I met Janet one day as she was walking her dog, invited her in for coffee and thus began a wonderful, rewarding friendship. Those were happy weekends when I looked up the street and saw a Silvertooth car. I knew then I would again hear more stories of Antelope's past. It had been a bustling sheep and cattle town of several hundred residents. Sometimes as many as three hundred cowponies were stabled in town overnight.

Ranch hands from neighboring spreads took advantage of the Silvertooth Saloon, and took great pleasure in galloping out of town with a whoopee after a night of revelry and unloading their pistols into the air as they rode.

Janet was a storehouse of tales of "oldtimes." Such as the

*Janet and Mildred Silvertooth growing up in
Antelope in the early 1930s*

Silvertooth House

Jessie Shay house (now John Silvertooth-Stewart House)

Donna's Pink House

days when the gypsies came each year and camped at the lower end of town, at which time she and her sister remained inside lest they be kidnapped. She remembers stories their mother told her about the Indians who regularly came through to gather wool from barbed wire fences where grazing sheep left it. Antelope was sheep country until sheepherders were impossible to hire. I still listen with keen interest to Janet's stories of small-town life, and I feel a little deprived of rural adventures, since I was reared in the city.

Another resident of Antelope to become a friend was Pat Cox, the schoolteacher at the two-room schoolhouse where she educated grades one through six. The postmaster's wife introduced us one Saturday at the post office stating that we should get acquainted since we were both alone. Another friendship formed.

In traveling through life, I have made many poor decisions, but in my selection of friends, I have carefully sifted through many folks in order to gather close to me those most kindly, well-mannered, generous, artistic and further endowed with those attributes that fulfill my criterion. My friends know that they have been lovingly chosen, and in return I let them know how privileged I am that they accept my hand in friendship.

No distance of place or lapse of time can lessen the friendship of those who are thoroughly persuaded of each other's worth.
—*Robert Southey*

Of what shall a man be proud, if he is not proud of his friends?
—*Robert Louis Stevenson*

Despite the diverse backgrounds of Antelope's populace—retired schoolteachers, ranchers, government employees, utility employees, mechanics—one common characteristic dominated all, a great spirit of independence.

The city of Antelope had no city tax base so generated no funds. When money was needed to pay for the street lights, pay for a new water pump, whatever was required, the folks would unite and throw their efforts into a fund-raising project, and it was the women who took this responsibility. They had the reputation for a one hundred mile radius as magnificent cooks so when word was passed that Antelope was having a cookout or fishfry in Meyer's Park, people came by the dozens to eat Annie Hick's baked beans, Margaret Hills' homemade ice cream, Frances Dickson's rolls and Darleen Osborne's pies. Margaret Mobley could roast a turkey to Craig Claiborne's delight, and anything else needed was aptly and amply supplied by Anna Meyer.

The city government was loose. No one desired to serve as mayor or on the city council. I questioned why such a small community was burdened with incorporation at all, but when I suggested disincorporation there were those who were aghast, arguing that the state revenue-sharing funds were needed, but these funds were dispensed on a per capita basis, and we only numbered forty. Had the residents known what was about to occur in that city's government, all would have quickly given up the charter!

Monthly council meetings oftentimes consisted of two motions, one to pay the bills and one to adjourn. Much of the necessary business including correspondence was often settled by the secretary and mayor before meetings. A system not in accordance with regulations, but it worked since so little concern was shown by anyone else. Rarely did a resident visit these meetings, although the notice was posted on the post office bulletin board.

One night widow Viola Wilson did request that her sister from a nearby ranch be allowed to pasture a couple of horses next to her house where the city property had grown into a fire hazard. She was told there was a very old law that required one dollar and fifty cents per month for such a privilege! Government was petty, and only selected ones were confronted with its restraints.

Stabling horses within the city limits did soon become the most antagonistic issue to face the council in many years. I had been drafted to a council position, so I read the zoning laws, laws implemented to improve the quality of life in the small town. Heretofore, Antelope's government had not adhered to these regulations with two exceptions: levy a building permit fee and require the specific setbacks for a new structure.

I endeavored to explain to those in favor of horses within the city that the zoning made no such provision. Some of us wanted to enforce the adopted regulations, while others chose to ignore them. A great argument ensued with one councilwoman transporting a retired cowpony into her backyard as a further silent demonstration. Ultimately, the assistant county planner was called to settle the dispute.

Yes. Antelope was a scrappy town, and its government relaxed, and unfortunately, sometimes it depended upon how much clout a resident had whether that person had to abide by the laws or not. Favoritism was a fact of life and squabbles were frequent. Life in Antelope would have been totally pleasing if the county seat had been the governing entity. Small-town politics pits neighbor against neighbor.

More of the period houses of Antelope

Anderson House

Butcher House

Connie's Place

Dickson House

Engblom House

Hensley House

Peterson House

Reynolds House

TWO

"Have you gotten your mail yet?" It was Donald Smith at my door. "No, I haven't been to the post office yet. Why?" "Well, you'll get an invitation to a posh party put on by those new folks who bought the Muddy Ranch. It's going to be at the Clarno Grange hall. Lots of free booze, baroque music, catered food, the works."

I didn't get an invitation and neither did most of us. Mayor Margaret Hill, Rancher Mobley, schoolteacher Pat Cox and the Muddy's outlying linefence neighbors were carefully selected.

That first party in the old grange hall with its buckled floor was just the beginning of a series of opulent celebrations to which people with clout and power, members of the media and politicians would be honored guests. Within eighteen months of their arrival in north central Oregon, some of the state capital crowd would be accepting free Rajneesh air flights to Rancho Rajneesh, there to be patronized and bedazzled.

In the meantime, twenty miles away in Antelope, residents felt consternation when two female sannyasins (followers of the master) came to town bare-breasted at about the same time in July of 1981 when *Time* magazine carried an advertisement to sell the writings of the Bhagwan Shree Rajneesh—writings which included films, audio and videocassettes. In that advertisement we read, "Sex, never repress it rather go deep into it with great clarity with great love. Go like an explorer. Search all the nooks and corners of your sexuality and you will be surprised and enriched and benefited . . . Sex is just the beginning not the end, but if you miss the beginning you will miss the end."

Imagine the excitement that day in our Podunk town as the postmistress showed us that July 20th issue of *Time* with an ad by our neighbor espousing sex as the true means to a greater enlightenment—an ad placed by the head of a powerful organization already well-settled on the remote cattle ranch!

We answered the ad. We wrote to Montclair, N.J. for the catalog and from the captions of the available materials we learned that Bhagwan dreamed of a closed city of 50,000 located in an obscure place where he could experiment with the egoless mind!

We read, "Unless you are ready to die for rebellion, you are not ready to be with a living master." That "die for rebellion" instilled fear in us as we remembered the mandatory death sentence of nine hundred Jim Jones' followers in Guyana.

Congressman Leo Ryan had been killed on the airstrip at Guyanasburg where he went to investigate complaints by Jones' followers. After his death, his daughter Shannon Jo, took his insurance money and joined the Rajneesh cult. With her initiation, she donned red clothes, placed a mala around her neck, (108 beads with a picture of Rajneesh attached.) Bhagwan Shree Rajneesh gave her a new birthdate and name, Ma Amrita Pritam. All females are Ma, and all males are Swami. Ma Pritam told the *Bend Bulletin,* "I think someone who becomes a sannyasin realizes the futility of pursuing materiality and learns there is more to life than living up to other people's expectations, like getting married, having children and a good job." *The Los Angeles Times* quoted her, "followers of the Bhagwan would kill themselves or others if he asked them to, but I don't think he would."

Who is this charismatic sex guru whose philosophy of "live, love, and laugh—celebrate life" who would "turn the world into a carnival of joy?" Rajneesh Chandra Mohan was born in India December 11, 1931 and was raised in the Jain religion. Upon the death his of grandfather, when he was seven, he became obsessed with death. He would rather follow a funeral cortege than go to a party.

At twenty-one he claimed to have experienced a mystical spiritual enlightenment. Enlightenment, according to him, is the ability to leave one's body and view it from a dis-

tance both in suffering and in death. Once that ability has
been attained, the chain of reincarnations is broken and such
is the goal.

He was university educated and considered highly intel-
lectual. He was a professor of philosophy, and in 1969 he began collecting Western followers on the streets of Bombay. It
was, in the sixties and seventies, the fad to find one's own
guru.

His technique was a combination of Eastern mysticism
and Western therapy. Those who followed him have been
described as: those whose self image stinks; those on the outs
with their own culture; intellects who have burned out in
their respective fields; those suffering great emotional stress
who wish to turn their back on the world.

As an example, a mother in Portland wrote, the "actions
without guilt" philosophy lured her guilt-ridden daughter to
leave her child and husband to join the Bhagwan's commune.

The backgrounds of the sannyasins knew no common
denominator as to race, nationality or social status. Even the
Queen of England's household knew grief due to the ability of
the Bhagwan to convert. Price Philip's cousin Welf and his
wife Princess Wibke moved to the commune in Poona taking
with them Princess Tania.

One month after Prince Philip had pleaded with his
cousin to quit the cult, Welf was killed in the commune with
a karate blow. Even so, his wife Wibke elected to remain.

When the commune folded, she moved to the ashram
(closed commune property) in Lucerne Valley, California, but
the Queen and Prince Philip arranged that Tania be rescued
while traveling through Germany on the way to America.
The Queen knew that adverse publicity could be the outcome, but insisted that Princess Tania's interests came above
everything else. As a spokesman for the German branch of
the Royal Family said, "We are anxious that Tania should be
brought up in an environment in keeping with her status."
(*The Globe*, January 5, 1982)

Once trapped, a cult devotee finds a complete authoritative and totalitarian state where unequivocal submission is demanded. Rajneesh allowed no one to question his decisions as proven in a speech he gave in Poona in 1978. A follower dared to question his reason for turning away a man at the gate, and a long castigating discourse followed which clearly discloses his dictatorial position. Here is part of that speech.

This is significant for everybody present here, and everybody who is going to be in any way related to me. I know who was turned away from the gate. And the man who has been turned away knows why he has been turned away from the gate. And it is none of your business to come into it.

This you have to understand absolutely; that whatsoever happens here, I may not come out of my room, but everything is perfectly known to me, is happening according to me. Please don't interfere.

This is not an ordinary place; everything is looked after. And if somebody needs a hit on the head, he is given it. You should not prevent it, otherwise, you will be coming into his growth too, and you will hinder him.

Laxmi (his secretary in India) never does anything on her own. She is a perfect vehicle. Laxmi has no idea; she simply listens and does. Whatsoever is said, she does.

Soon we will be becoming a bigger commune and thousands of people will be coming. The moment you give a suggestion to me, you are disconnected from me. This is not going to be a democracy. Your votes will never be taken. You become part of it with that knowledge—that whatsoever I decide is absolute. If you don't choose that way, you are perfectly happy to leave. People are prevented from entering, but nobody is prevented from leaving.

This place will never be according to you. This place is to change you; it is not to be according to you, and these are the beginnings. Who are you to know what is right and what is wrong? And who are you to ask for the reason?

This is a place where many things will never be according to you. You have to fall in tune with things. Many questions have been coming to me. Somebody participates in a group and writes, "Why is there so much violence in the encounter group?" In the West, encounter groups have limitations, because the encounter group leader has limitations. He can only go so far. Here we don't believe in any boundaries.

The moment you surrender and become an initiate, a sannyasin, that surrender has to be total. Just live a few months in that total surrender and you will see—it is alchemical, it transforms you.

Some people come and they think, "What has happened to these people? Do they understand? Have they become apathetic, indifferent?" No. They have learned. Slowly, slowly they have learned that whatsoever happens is happening according to a plan, a device. There is some hidden pattern in it, and nobody except me knows what that hidden pattern is. So you cannot go to Laxmi; she simply asks me what is to be done and she does it.

If you are to be part of this commune, you have to understand this, you have to relax, you have to stop judging. Soon, after a few months of relaxation you will be able to understand. That's what has happened to the older sannyasins.

How does a cult leader gather followers? Few people set out to become a cult member, and even if they should be susceptible, unless they have an encounter with a recruiter their chances of following a cult leader are slight. These recruiters are skillful propagandists, overly friendly, often offer solutions to complex problems, and so it was with the large public relations staff under the direction of Rajneesh. They pictorially and verbally painted an Utopic life-style promising a life of complete abandonment, freedom from any responsibility, freedom of guilt regardless of actions, complete safety from the world without, a storehouse of organically grown food and underground housing where only his followers will emerge into the new world following the worldwide holocaust he predicted would occur in 1997. The safety of his Rajneeshees is assured because they will generate enough "positive energy" to avoid any catastrophic event.

I cannot rely on the prognoses of a guru whose every ut-

terance was designed to antagonize, mesmerize and prosely-
tize; however, if I could believe his prognostication of global
annihilation would come to pass, as accurately as his predic-
tion about Acquired Immune Deficiency Syndrome, I would
alter my life in such a manner as to spend it and my last dollar
simultaneously.

It was in March of 1985 that he declared that two-thirds
of the world population was threatened by AIDS. In his paper, the *Rajneesh Times,* he admonished his followers, "If you
are ready and can drop sex altogether through understanding
and without repression, this is the safest protection against
the disease. Or remain with the same partner, merge with the
same partner, move more and more into intimacy and less
into sexual activity."

Cult leaders are prolific writers, and following the destruction of civilization, his three-hundred-fifty volumes
were to be the ABC's of the new civilization with
Rajneeshpuram its gene bank!

The Bhagwan and Hitler have been compared by several
writers. Hitler experimented with the body and dreamed of
creating the pure Aryan race. Bhagwan experimented with
the mind and dreamed of discovering from whence enlightenment comes. His closed city of 50,000 was to be the guinea
pig's cage.

He was thwarted in his attempt to build his many-people
city in his native land, even though his business agent Laxmi
had located two desirable plots, one four-hundred acres and
the other two-thousand acres. The Indian government would
not permit rezoning of the agricultural land. India, with its
starving millions, protects its farmland.

His ashram was extremely overcrowded. He needed
more land. The local citizens looked with disdain upon the
orange-clothed sannyasins—many of whom plied the trade of
prostitution. India is a most chaste country, where even holding hands on the street is frowned upon, and so the "rich
man's guru" became an outcast in the country of gurus due to
his liberal moral teachings.

Local landlords did profit from followers by charging exorbitant rental fees. One wealthy landholder rented to them an old castle in which followers began making scent-free soap and the beaded malas. Adjacent to the castle was a water well which was not included in the rental agreement, but water being scarce, armed sannyasins took control of it. A young Ma was sent to the home of the landlord as a messenger, and when he drove her back to the ashram, she began shouting accusations of rape. She exposed a bruised breast—a tactic used to forestall his lawsuit over the legal seizure of the well, but the landlord could not be blackmailed. He took the Rajneeshees to court and was victorious.

In May of 1981 Rajneesh left Poona with eighteen of his trusted workers. His departure was sudden—just before members of his hierarchy were to be indicted for arson, insurance fraud and false accusations of rape. He left India owing his government millions of rupees in back taxes.

With the absence of the leaders of the Poona commune, seven-thousand followers were left adrift. Without guidance and deprived of emotional security, many committed suicide, and others more fortunate found their way home to family, and some became residents of the local mental institution.

Indian tax authorities attached Rajneesh foundation bank accounts in an attempt to recover some of the overdue taxes, but the accounts yielded only a fraction of the amount owed. "The titles to trust-owned property, moreover, are in a deliberately muddled and confusing state." (*India Today,* June 15, 1982)

We have known many Rajneesh entities beginning with Rancho Rajneesh, but the major branches may be sorted out in this way: The Rajneesh Investment Corporation (RIC) was the business branch with all properties owned in that name. The church organization was known as Rajneesh Foundation International (RFI) and was registered that way as nonprofit with the federal government. The Rajneesh Neo-Sannyasins Commune (RNSC) leased its commune property from RIC. In London on Whimple Street Rajneesh Services International (RSI) had an office, and RSI held a mortgage loan on all real and personal properties, so it appears all titles here were just as muddled as their holdings in Poona.

It was Sheela Silverman, Rajneesh's new secretary and business agent, who bought the Muddy Ranch in North central Oregon. The sixty-four thousand acres, remote and inaccessible, was precisely what Rajneesh dreamed of owning. She paid one and one-half million down on the six million dollar price.

The Muddy Ranch is twenty miles from Antelope. It was well populated with Rajneeshees by August 1981, but their mail-order business was still functioning out of Montclair, New Jersey, because adequate telephone service could not be immediately supplied to the ranch.

RIC purchased their first Antelope property, a parcel that had been for sale before they arrived. A double-wide mobile home and a small commercial building known as "the rock shop" became their new mail order headquarters. They applied for a business license from Antelope city government, and it was granted without hesitation since rumors had circulated that a Chicago attorney had been flown in to sue the city if the license was denied. That was just a rumor, but in the months to come numerous lawsuits would be inflicted upon the local folks as they attempted to thwart the colonization of Rajneeshees in central Oregon. "Rajneesh has a sixty-million dollar cashflow." We heard that many times. Was it rumor or fact? People sometimes equate wealth with honor and poverty with crime. Perhaps Bhagwan counted on that viewpoint. Sheela told us later many of the rumors were instigated by her in order to "give empty heads something to think about."

The first of dozens of meetings to be held regarding the red-clothed followers occurred in August 1981 in the auditorium of the schoolhouse. Officials from both Wasco and Jefferson county were in attendance. The judge from Jefferson county opened the discussion by telling us the Rajneeshees were there, they were legal, and they were not to be harassed. "Do you have any questions?"

About fifty unreds were present, and all were reluctant to speak, given the judge's opening lines. Finally a rancher's wife broke the awkward silence, and said she did wonder why they needed building permits for thirty-five mobile homes to house fifty ranch hands when her husband successfully operated an equally large ranch with one live-in family and a couple of extra riders when cattle were moved from one range to another.

The woman in charge of Wasco County's Planning Department was there and stated that she was handling the area as a subdivision; when questioned how she could grant permits for a subdivision on farm-zoned land, she replied "subdivision" was a slip of the tongue.

We also told the judge the mobile homes headed for the Muddy had six bedrooms but no kitchen and so did not qualify as a single-family unit. (One had been parked in front of my house, and I had checked it out.) He quickly told us he had visited Sheela's lovely home with a spacious round kitchen and all the houses were alike. In support of their life-style, he added with a grin, that the old laying hens would die a natural death, because these people did not believe in killing anything.

The tenor of that first meeting prevailed at similar meetings for nearly eighteen months with members of public media and politicians alike accepting as truths what Rajneeshees said; whereas, the residents of Antelope quickly learned within six weeks after arrival that their *actions* not their *words* provided the truth.

It was long past the planting time in the valley when they began to till the land, but the Wasco County planner granted them a building permit for a large barn for "produce storage." We knew it held the mail order stock. We encouraged the lady planner, Dorothy Sodersterom Brown to investigate, but she did not.

In the middle of December Bob and Darleen Osborne received a Christmas card from Chattanooga, Tennessee, and enclosed was a full page report of Rancho Rajneesh. It read like a travelog. Included in the newspaper pictures was the very building in question, and the caption below it read, "Holding Area—Under a portrait of Bhagwan, workers toil in a warehouse that houses videotapes, cassette tapes and books of the guru's messages which are sold worldwide."

We delivered that article to the planner. Again we asked her to investigate. She continued issuing building permits to them, numbering over fifty-seven, until she retired in May 1982. Then young Dan Durow, assistant planner, replaced her.

He granted no permits that were not in accordance with the law—no permits for buildings unrelated to farm operations; furthermore, he made premise visits to photograph their new buildings while under construction and measure them for any deviation from the original specifications. On one of his visits to the ranch, he found a Rajneeshee truck stalled on the narrow farm road. For some unknown mechanical reason, it could not be moved out of his way. Eventually, it became necessary for him to be accompanied by a county sheriff.

In retribution for his adherence to county laws, the Rajneeshees firebombed the Wasco County Planning Office in January 1985, destroying many of the county's records.

THREE

Donald and I had delightful time getting acquainted. He found out I liked to photograph and paint old buildings, so in a four-wheel drive pickup he chartered new roads through the back country, mushing through green meadows, bumping through dry and wet creekbeds as he delivered me from one old farmstead to another.

I learned that the many thousand-acre ranch of today is an aggregate of yesterday's homesteads. If the weathered buildings were hidden in a draw, their location could easily be spotted from a distance by the ever popular poplar trees grown wondrously tall over the years. All homesteaders must have loved these quick-growing trees for windbreaks and welcome shade. Old orchards still exist looking quite unkempt but still productive, providing prunes and apples for birds and coyotes and for those local folks who know where to find them.

We saw Maupin Butte. We traveled Tub Springs and bounced through the sagebrush to Grub Hollow where I quickly painted an old shack that had settled comfortably into the rocks with its door open as if still beckoning to a weary wayfarer. We saw the area known as Sore Foot, named for its propensity to lame a bull every year.

It was the Herman place where I fantasized about life at the turn of the century as I walked around the smoke house which could have been a Chick Sales outhouse but for its unusual height. The sidewalls of the Herman house had given up and allowed the roof to list awkwardly, but the upstairs was still discernible. Rusted, open-coiled bedsprings were in one corner and an infant bed of iron was nearby. What graphic mental pictures I built with these old props.

On these adventurous trips I gathered bits of harness, old enamel utensils and pieces of horsedrawn machinery— machinery which at one time had helped to propagate and reap crops. Horseshoes were a lucky find, too. Donald started his own collection of buggy steps. I nailed my treasures of by-gone days on the back wall of the woodshed for all passersby to see. This collage I called "courageous art" since it required some courage to suggest it was art in any form.

Family entertainment when I was child was a picnic lunch and a trip to Multnomah falls via the Mount Hood Loop Highway. Wherever we went my brother and I read the big barns with their own signs advertising: Chew Mail Pouch Tobacco, Bull Durham, Lydia Pinkham's Compound, and Carter's Little Liver Pills.

I had grown up with the hidden desire to paint such a sign, but never had the building on which to put it. A fruit cellar stood behind the pink house and had a gable facing Baird Street. One day I disclosed my childhood dream to a neighbor who thought, as I did, that Lydia Pinkham's Compound would be most apropos. I did it, and it still remains, but the mural I had painted below it now hangs in the Riverside Hotel in Maupin.

"God, I love you. I'll do the yard work, help around the house, and I'm a helluva cook. Will you marry me?" He surprised me right in the middle of a plate of chow mein. Although I had discovered that Donald was a real social charmer, compassionate, and honest, I also knew our life-styles were quite different, so I expressed my gratitude and suggested he ask me again in six or eight months; however, his persistence that we marry before winter prevailed.

We were wed September 11, 1981. "Night and Day have decided to merge for a lifetime of sunny afternoons," was the notice I mailed to friends. He moved into the pink house with the white gingerbread. It seemed the eighty-five-year-old building had been restored for just such a love affair. We were fortunate to share the autumn of our lives in that house in Antelope.

While honeymooning in Reno, we enjoyed dinner-theater entertainment. Sitting two tables from us was a most handsome Hindu couple—he in his turban headdress and she in a luxurious silk sari. I thought how exciting it would be to speak with them, so when she left the table, I followed her. At a convenient time, I told her that I lived in a small town where one of her countrymen now lived. "Do you know Shree Rajneesh?" I asked. "Yes," she responded. "I live in his town of Poona." Then she added that she saw my town on television in London just before leaving. "Why did he arrive on a stretcher?" she asked. "He was in good health." I felt that last comment was meant to tell me that he was not honest.

Donald was of great encouragement to me in my art and was content to sit and read in his pickup while I sketched in some remote spot. In the long winter evenings we played cribbage and sometimes rancher Bob Hastings and his wife Pearl joined us for a meal and highly contested games of pinochle. Bob had been reared in our house so was quite at home.

On the weekends when Chet and Raye Reynolds were in town at their house two blocks "uptown," meaning up the hill, we joined them for dinner and more cards. Chet was soon to retire, and they both looked forward to moving into their

Photo courtesy *Bend Bulletin*

Donald and Donna Smith with Tizzy Lish

Antelope Cafe and Store

restored Antelope home.

So our early wedded days passed pleasantly. It was a new venture, and even though Donald had warned me, "you have got to understand, I never remember birthdays, holidays and anniversaries" I adjusted to that. It was the constant surveillance of us by the Rajneeshees and daily photographing of us and our property that I could not adjust to. We would soon be thrust into the eye of Hurricane Rajneesh and emerge quite different people due to the adjustments we would be forced to make in order to survive emotionally.

Shortly before the arrival of Bhagwan Shree Rajneesh, I resigned my council position. I told the mayor I moved to Antelope to paint, not to settle local disputes. Little did I know then how involved I would become at a later date.

Mayor Margaret Hill found the demands of the red people and their threats of lawsuits most distressful and gradually she delegated the weight of city government to Donald who took the responsibility in stride. Gentle person that the mayor was, she was in constant fear of being the target of a lawsuit. That fear inhibited her from implementing some aggressive actions at the onset. She would later be sued anyway.

Donald liked the challenge, but the time would come when he also would suffer from the pressure of the Bhagwan's boot as his insidious machine walked in and took what he wanted, always using the laws to his advantage. Donald did the mayor's legwork, and the council members looked to him to make the decisions.

It was on November 4, 1981 in the Dalles County courthouse that the cornerstone for the Bhagwan's empire was set in place. The Rajneesh had petitioned the county court for the right to vote themselves a city at the Muddy ranch, and everyone from the Antelope Valley traveled to the county seat to oppose that request. The Sannyasans got there first. Each bench held Sannyasans with spaces left in between for us. Their sophisticated camera equipment was in place. This was our first introduction to their determination to always videotape and always eavesdrop all conversations at all meetings.

Oregon has solid land use laws. When they petitioned Wasco County for election rights to incorporate a city on farm land, we were convinced that the laws would prevail; however, we didn't know then that Judge Rick Cantrell, head of the three man county commission, had made a deal with the Rajneeshees—a deal to sell fifty-nine head of cattle to them. They had made the arrangements on October 25 with the purchase price in the amount of $17,540—the precise amount of the judge's farm loan at the U.S. National Bank of The Dalles. The cattle were delivered after the hearing, delivered in the middle of the night without benefit of a brand inspection.

Brand inspector Buck Hodges made an unannounced visit to the ranch, couldn't locate eleven of the fifty-nine head, but did find the judge visiting his new friends. Frequently we in Antelope observed the judge driving through in his county car on his way to the ranch. Several months later, the judge was sent or volunteered to go to Nigeria on a church mission, a timely departure inasmuch as Wasco County citizens had begun his recall.

Unique Oregon political history was made on that November 4th in the courthouse. No help from the state capital arrived to oppose this colonization on farmland, although the state Land Conservation and Development Commission is authorized to police the land use ordinances.

Testimony was presented by many people opposing the city. Several ranchers, who were more at home in the field repairing a tractor than in the courthouse giving a speech, made pertinent and succinct arguments. When the Rajneeshee attorney claimed the land to be built upon was classed number seven soil, "unsuited to forage crops," rancher Frank McNamee stated, "Pretty hard to tell a cow grazing on seven soil that she can't eat there."

Donald gave a researched presentation referring to the Oregon Revised Statute prohibiting urban growth on agricultural land. The Muddy Ranch was zoned Essential Farm Use, (EFU). The land use watchdog group, 1,000 Friends of Oregon, (founded by ex-governor Tom McCall) was represented by Paul Gerhardt who delivered clear testimony as to the law, i.e. necessary urban growth must be adjacent to an already urbanized area.

A non-Rajneeshee, Grant Russell, who spoke in favor of the city in the outback, was a salesman who had realized considerable monetary gain through sales of heavy construction equipment to the group, and he realized the potential for even greater economic gain in the future if a city of 50,000 was to be developed on the rangeland.

Present that day, in the employ of the Rajneesh, was Edward Sullivan who had assisted in the original drafting of Oregon's land use laws. Whatever their endeavor, the Rajneeshees engaged only the experts to argue their cause. I must give them credit for their strategic ability. They gathered the most noted Generals before their opponents knew there was going to be a war.

Three county officials heard many hours of testimony that infamous November 4th: Virgil Ellett, he seemed to sleep through it all, Jim Comini and the cattle-selling judge, Rick Cantrell. It was a two to one vote in favor of the Rajneeshees voting themselves a city in the sagebrush. This same two to one vote prevailed at future hearings until the judge's missionary trip. Commissioner Comini told me that we could never dissuade him. "He's committed to them!"

Rajneeshee photographers were active panning the audience that day. Raye Reynolds sat next to me and covered her face with each turn of the lens. After that, Rajneeshee photographers singled her out to photograph at subsequent meetings. I preferred to smile and wave.

Soon they began taking our pictures when we stepped outside our homes in Antelope. They took pictures of us as we went into the cafe and the post office. They photographed us in our yards. One day they followed the movements of one of my elderly neighbors as he mowed the park. When he moved to the other side of the property to escape them, they traveled the street and continued to harass him until they drove him into his house in a state of nerves. He had lost his niece to a cult and was ever fearful of these cultists.

It was now that I knew I couldn't remain there. Before we were married, Donald had promised me we would move from their midst and leave Rajneesh and his relatives behind, but when I reminded him of his promise, he said he wanted to stay and fight. He enjoyed the battle, but I did not enjoy his participation, which kept him on the road between The Dalles and Madras weekly. He used his hours at home escaping between the covers of books. He read fiction incessantly. He preferred fiction to any nonfictional conversations, so little verbal exchange took place between us.

Finally I realized he could cope with the red machine no better than I. He became resentful of my accuracy in predicting "what's gonna happen next," and adding to the stress in our home was the constant stream of media people who came in pairs—a writer and a photographer.

Donald had been an amateur stage actor and emoted very well and very happily. When I put a note on the front door that members of the media were not welcome, with the exception of Tom Stimmel of the <u>Oregon Journal</u> and David Cash of the <u>Bend Bulletin</u>, he found and removed it.

David Cash was a favorite newsperson of mine. He came to interview us one day, and I was somewhat testy due to some misquotes in the <u>Oregonian</u>, so I admonished him to be precisely accurate. I further told him that if he quoted me at all to be sure and say that I said, "Sheela lied." He did.

FOUR

The first two Rolls Royces belonging to the Bhagwan arrived fully equipped with bulletproof glass. Did he expect violence? For weeks he careened over the country roads at breakneck speeds which, on at least three occasions, put him a ditch. One time he traveled a dry creek bed at the expense of the undercarriage of his car. On another one of his flights into the sagebrush, Margaret and Phil Hill discovered him sitting off the road and inquired if he was all right. He sat motionless, faced directly ahead and refused to acknowledge their offer to help. A strange encounter! After several citations from the sheriff for his reckless driving, we observed a pilot car that preceded him on his daily drives off the ranch. Soon he had a rear guard also.

His jaunts were precisely three o'clock every day. He drove through the end of our town on his way to Madras. Those followers who worked in the mail order business in Antelope would line both sides of the road and wave arms wildly overhead and jump up and down and generally gyrate.

Donald took some pictures of them (we used our cameras, too). After that, they changed their stance and clasped their hands in a prayerful manner and smiled and nodded as he passed. Some were seen crying.

The Bhagwan's daily trip took him to Madras, where he turned around for the homeward flight. Mardo Jiminez, a local conservative Baptist preacher, began meeting his entourage there. Many of his parishioners accompanied him as well as sightseers. Soon a massive crowd gathered to hear the ambitious attempt to convert Rajneeshees from Rajneeshism to Christianity with vigorous delivery. Jefferson county sheriff, Ham Perkins, asked Sheela to see to it that Bhagwan took a different route in order to avert mayhem.

Again his photographers were on hand. The cameras caught scruffy looking cowboys with angry faces and sometimes an obscene gesture at close camera range. Did the cam-

Photo courtesy *Bend Bulletin*/Doug Bradley

The Bhagwan waved to followers along the dusty road as he left for his daily spin into Madras.

eramen antagonize the local Madras folks? Did they edit the video tapes to their desire? I don't know, but much shouting and shaking of fists was caught by the photographers.

We in Antelope, thirty-eight miles away, knew his destination, but none of us were in Madras at that time, and I had not known of the immensity of the crowd until a year later when the Bhagwan's attorney Swami Niren entered that choreographed movie of complete hysteria as evidence against me at my trial.

I was mortified that such behavior had taken place. No one from Antelope took part or condoned such action and, after all, Madras residents had their own feelings of fear and resentment towards the red people.

Photo courtesy The Dalles *Weekly Reminder*

*Falling to their knees, two sannyasins are apparently
overwhelmed by the passing of Bhagwan in his Rolls-Royce.*

It was January of 1982 that I met Ma Anand Sheela, a.k.a. Sheela Silverman, the Bhagwan's secretary, in the home of my neighbors Arthur and Annie Hicks. They lived across the street from the mail order offices in a modern mobile home. Also on their lot was the oldest house in town which is the only house in Antelope listed with the state as an historical landmark to be preserved. The Rajneeshees coveted these buildings with the sleeping space they offered, especially since the winter weather made the twenty mile trip from the ranch to their offices in town precarious on the farm roads which couldn't support the many heavy vehicles.

In the first seven months following their arrival, it cost Wasco County over twenty thousand dollars to maintain just the one county road that cuts through the Muddy Ranch.

Rajneeshee office workers would often drop in at the Hickses with homemade pastries and bread. Arthur said he got quite sick one day after eating a tart. I couldn't help but wonder what the Bhagwan would like to do to him. Arthur never wanted any of them in his house and was adamantly opposed to selling them anything. He had a genuine fear of these people, unlike his wife, Annie, who was hospitable to the young women and welcomed their company—perhaps because she was a near shut in due to crippling arthritis.

One day during one of our visits, in walked Sheela with office manager Ma Shanti Bhadra. Annie introduced us, though we already knew each other from public meetings. In the conversation that ensued, Sheela said the state attorney general was a personal friend of hers. "You mean Dave Frohmayer?" I asked. She made no acknowledgment, "Then you knew him before you moved to Oregon?" another question. "No," she replied. "To become a friend takes many years of wear and not a short seven months," I told her. She obviously resented my challenging remarks, flipped her head around to Annie and asked "Who are the people at the cafe who said we are stockpiling guns?" I realized after I left for home that her question was meant for my ears in the hopes I might divulge any firsthand information I might have about trucks carrying guns to the ranch.

It was Mrs. Peterson, one of my aloof neighbors, who told me that she had spoken with a man whose brother was one of the three truck drivers who delivered armaments to the Muddy. They had passed our house in the night, and night traffic was very intrusive in the cemetery-quiet town, but I knew nothing about those trucks. Later we learned that Rancho Rajneesh was a veritable fortress.

A Rajneesh doctor came calling on Annie one day, took her temperature and asked health-oriented questions. It seems Shanti Bhadra had found her on the couch earlier. He was most solicitous, and his bill for forty dollars arrived soon after.

We told her not to pay it. She didn't. She was a wise and moderately wealthy lady with a quick wit. Some of my neighbors refused to visit with her, said she was senile and passing information to the Rajneeshees, but they also said that she had been a madam of a bawdy house. Annie and I had a hearty laugh over that. She was wonderfully determined, had traveled more than most of the local folks, and I always left her home with a warm, happy feeling.

Darleen and I were drinking coffee in Annie's kitchen one day when two female sannyasins came in to ask for the key for the old historic house in order to look at the pumpkins Arthur had stored inside. "The ranch cook might buy them," one said. Annie gave them the key. Darleen told her they weren't interested in the pumpkins but rather they wanted to investigate from the inside and see how many people could sleep there.

Two weeks later Annie told us they offered her a check for twenty thousand dollars as a down payment on both houses. She said Sheela handed her the check, a contract and a gold pen she said was worth five thousand dollars. Annie returned the pen, the check and the unsigned contract. Arthur and Annie didn't want to leave Antelope.

The hierarchy persisted, and three weeks later Annie did agree to sell the old house for cash with the stipulation that their mobile home would also be bought with cash by that summer. As Annie put it, "I can't live next to those gurus." Quickly, several of Annie's "gurus" began emptying the historical building. Besides winter vegetables, Arthur had the house packed with old furniture and antique artifacts. He had need of time to sort through these household goods, but the gurus had their orders and couldn't be deterred. Annie telephoned the mayor in tears; the mayor called Donald who called the Wasco County Sheriff who halted the hasty removal of Hicks's personal property.

Swami Jayananda, a.k.a. John Shelfer and Sheela's new husband also visited Annie. On one of his visits she was bewailing the taxes she would pay in 1982 due to the interest accrued on notes. All of us had heard that John had been a banker before accompanying his wife to central Oregon, so Annie foolishly asked him for advice with investments.

Following that conversation with him, Sheela began urging Annie to move to the ranch promising her maidservants and a new mobile home at a very reasonable price.

Arthur and Annie had already bought a lot in Fossil thirty-nine miles away, and twice she told Sheela, "No." The third time she told Sheela, "No, we are not moving to the ranch. We're going to Fossil, and whatever this thing has been between us is ended. The people in Fossil don't want any of you gurus over there." With her last refusal, Sheela told her it made no difference anyway since her life expectancy was no more than two years!

When Annie told me how Sheela would coerce her to move to the ranch, I remembered a deduction that Darleen and I had made shortly after the Madras hospital hired two Rajneeshee nurses. We believed that the nurses had been placed there for reasons other than salary, and the first of November 1981, I got a telephone call that confirmed our suspicions.

A woman who was a paraplegic and also crippled with arthritis called me from Madras. She was obviously frightened as she told me about a visit two Rajneeshees made to her home soon after she had been released from the hospital. She was expecting a friend who had often visited on Thursday evenings, and so when she heard a knock she opened the door to be confronted by a swami and a Ma. The female stepped in, and the Swami followed her after looking up and down the walk.

They looked around her living room—commented on a new television set, and then asked her questions about her income while at the same time promising her that a cure for the arthritis existed at the ranch where she could live in a new mobile home and eat specially grown food, raised organically with healing properties. She said they told her they would be back before Christmas to move her. It was the first week in November.

I, too, asked her questions regarding her income. When I learned that she existed on meager funds I assured her she need not worry. Rajneeshees would not be back. They were only interested in those folks who could contribute handsomely to their economy. The nurses in the hospital were a good source of information regarding the release of patients with a questionable lifespan.

When Sheela's attempts to move Annie and Arthur to the ranch fell on deaf ears, and she told Annie she would likely die within two years anyway, an abrupt end came to any rapport that may have existed between them; however, she did make an unexpected and unpleasant visit to Annie in Fossil on March 11, 1982.

Just before moving to Fossil, Annie told me Sheela said she was going to buy enough property in Antelope to control the taxes, and John said those folks who drug their feet about selling would later be forced to sell their home at his price. Four days later I wrote those statements as she dictated them to me, and she signed the paper. Our city attorney requested this be done.

Given the aggressiveness of the Bhagwan's hierarchy and these threats to control the economics of Antelope, it seemed prudent to return the city charter to the state and thereby remove the political body before the next general election in November 1982.

Strangely enough, when I suggested to one of the old-timers we had better get rid of the government, she asked me if we weren't running scared, and "are they really that bad?" Yes, there were those who could not, or would not, believe what had already happened nor could they imagine what the future held. Were they not equipped emotionally to think about disaster, or were they sure that our government officials would step in and take charge before we were forced from our homes? I don't know.

Nor did I know the importance of Annie's signed statement until a town meeting was called on March tenth, and our attorney, Keith Mobley, announced that we could ask permission from the state to hold a special election on April fifteenth.

Now the wheels were really in motion to disincorporate Antelope!

On March eleventh I called Annie in Fossil, and I told of the town meeting and its outcome. "It's quite possible the Rajneeshees will harass you in some way, so be prepared." I told her. She said Sheela had already been there and had insisted she sign yet another statement stating she did not know what it was that she had signed in the first place. Annie said she refused, but Sheela would not take no for an answer. Annie called the local retired Wheeler County District Attorney to come to her assistance. He did. He advised Sheela to "head on out, or I'll sue you for a million dollars."

He did not wait to see Sheela leave, and Sheela doggedly insisted that Annie sign a retraction. Annie finally wearily acquiesced.

FIVE

We knew the Bhagwan came to Oregon with a plan to build a city of fifty thousand, and under the guise of farmers they moved in fifty, two hundred and eighty and then over two thousand "ranch hands".

For eight months some of us had written our elected officials both at the state and federal levels requesting a full investigation of Bhagwan. Few replies were forthcoming, and those promised no action. They simply expressed concern. It was not popular at that time to oppose this minority, and we, the affected electorate, were few and lived in a place unheard of by most politicians.

I'm reminded of a telephone conversation I had with an official in the Portland office of the Federal Labor Relations Bureau in which I requested someone from that office visit the ranch and determine what kind of work the children were doing and under what working conditions. "How do you know they are working?" he asked. "Because Sheela said even the children of five work everyday, and I read it in the Oregonian." "Who's Sheela?" and finally, "We'd have to send someone way over there from here." I found the Department of Labor in Washington, D.C. "way over there" much more concerned about the Oregon children.

The helplessness and utter frustration of it all embraced me like a shroud. Anguish was visible on the faces of my neighbors who had chosen this once peaceful town for their last abode. In despair, I sent the following letter to the staff of Sixty Minutes television program; after all, they did investigative work on bizarre occurrences.

"*The Death of a City: you might call it. Tonight the city council of Antelope, Oregon voted to hold a special election for the purpose of disincorporation and thus thwart the attempt of the followers of the Bhagwan Shree Rajneesh to gain control of the city government next November when three council positions will be vacated, also the mayor's post.*

The cult has purchased enough residential property within the city limits of Antelope to control it through its registered voters. We feel their candidate's success is assured through numerical superiority. Their second in command, Sheela Silverman, has said, "I will give people around here something to think about. I will own so much property that I can control the taxes here."

It was June of 1981 that the Rajneesh Meditation International, a nonprofit organization then based in Montclair, New Jersey, bought the old cattle ranch known as the Muddy, and in a July issue of Time was their advertisement (enclosed) which startled all of us.

We have been harassed and intimidated and frightened as we read of their therapy sessions aimed at developing the mindless and egoless man. Sessions that break bones, destroy minds, and permit sexual attacks at will. Religious attainment through sexual freedom is one of their philosophies.

The folks who live in this oasis in the high desert country of central Oregon are of different backgrounds and settled here to go their independent ways in this Shangri-La many miles from the abominations of a large metropolis. Before Rajneesh moved his headquarters here, the most worrisome item on the city agenda was whether or not another horse could be stabled within the city limits. This still is cattle country with a real John Wayne look-a-like as postmaster.

Yes, you could say that tonight determined the death of Antelope with its honored charter of 1902. A death warrant signed by the very ones that love her most in order to preserve the constitutional rights of the few remaining residents. The Rajneesh and his first in command, Sheela Silverman, are non-citizens, yet they wield the unreal power to turn our lives into a daily nightmare.

What I have told you thus far is but a smattering of what I could tell you, but to provoke your curiosity is my aim. Enclosed are some of the data I have collected, with the very best to follow as soon as it returns to me from Portland.

My husband and I have been the most vociferous in the

attack against this cult, though many have written our con-
gressmen and state officials asking for a full investigation of
this group's activities in Poona, India and Montclair, New Jer-
sey. Only polite letters of concern are received in return.

Just tonight since I began this letter to you I have learned
that the cult has asked for a permit to hold a "festival of the
moon" celebration here in July with attendance over five
thousand. What will that do to this sleepy little town of
twenty households?

If you are not sufficiently curious, I would add that our
mayor, Mrs. Margaret Hill, cannot hold a lady's extension
meeting without the cult accusing her of holding an illegal
town meeting, nor can the local fellows visit in Al Kuhlman's
Antelope garage without them taking pictures of those who
come and go with accusations of another clandestine meet-
ing.

You see, they bought our little eight-stool cafe where we
used to gather to gossip, etc.

It truly is a tragic tale entitled "The death of a City."

Soon their scout, Barbara Baylor, arrived at my door. A
much out-of-place New Yorker, with an easy charm. She
stepped into the parlor with the grace of a Fifth Avenue cou-
turier, but soon we sat at the kitchen table, where I filled her
stomach with peach pie and her ears with alarming tales of
pending disaster for Antelope. The entire crew arrived a
month later. Ed Bradley was the moderator. He asked Margaret Hill, Donald and I to sit on the front bench in the 1897
Antelope church. Attorney Garry McMurry arrived and was
included. Mr. Bradley asked each of us the same questions.

In the final airing, Donald and I were seen but not heard
which possibly protected me from a lawsuit at that time, since
I spoke out more aggressively than the others. One question
Mr. Bradley posed, "If the Bhagwan were to leave now, would
you be happy?" The others answered yes, but I said, "No, because wherever he goes there will be chaos."

Most of the airtime was devoted to the ranch, and the selective exposure was splendid. People throughout the nation responded sympathetically sending money for Antelope's legal expenses.

In the meantime, the Rajneeshees were working swiftly. With the disincorporation election imminent, their business agent began making offers to buy more houses. His mother had named him David Knapp. Bhagwan named him Swami Krishna Deva, but to us he was always City Slick. He was in charge of purchasing real estate in town. He was the Rajneesh spokesman at all Antelope meetings and the most disliked of all those with whom we were in close proximity. Antelopeans particularly disliked City Slick.

Bhagwan's people needed sufficient places to sleep within the city in order to effect the plan to assume control of the government. Oldtime residents were divided in their feelings to sell or not to sell. Many wanted to leave in order to extricate themselves from Rajneeshee harassment, but they did not want to sell to the machine. How could folks move away if they could not recover their investment? Others elected to remain and wait for state help to come riding over the mountain from the capital, but the Governor's Aide had already told us, "It's a local problem."

One oldtime family living in the largest Victorian home in town moved, stripping their home of everything including the wall-to-wall carpeting. They were certain the Rajneeshees would soon own every building, and they were leaving nothing behind.

Another family chose to move to nearby Madras and keep their property with the hope of returning one day.

Raye and Chet originally thought they would hold out as long as emotionally possible, but Ray's dedicated opposition to the cult affected her health, and the quality of their marriage. "We have had more arguments this past year than in all our thirty-eight years." They gave up and sold their house. Chet had urged Raye to stop attending the meetings, but she could not give up her cause to confront the Rajneeshees.

There are those of us who endeavor, no matter how Gargantuan the task, to correct wrongs wherever they are found. There are those who are aware of these ills and are content to sit back and observe the dedicated ones do all the work, and still others fail to see anything wrong, because their entire world begins and ends at their own front gate.

City Slick negotiated with Bob and Darleen for their house across from the school. It was a mobile home onto which Bob had built a cozy addition of old barn boards, and that family room, complete with a sheepherder's stove, was my most favorite place to visit.

One day Darleen and I were sharing thoughts in her barnboard hideaway when suddenly tears welled up in her eyes, and she told me she and Bob had sat up all night discussing what to do. She was losing weight, had no appetite, and he had been unable to sleep for weeks. They capitulated to the Rajneeshees and sold their home.

They moved a mile out of town and continued to pick up mail in town, but she has never looked upon her house since they moved. Should you visit her today, you would feel the same despair she has known as you listen to her story of shattered dreams and destroyed expectations for the future.

Widow Viola Wilson sold. City Slick did not give her the customary thirty days in which to vacate, because they needed occupancy by April 15th. Instead, they told her, "Be out by April 3rd, or we'll make other arrangements."

City Slick also made an appointment with me to see the pink house. I asked Donald what he thought I should do. He advised me to sell to them. "Might be the last opportunity to sell to anyone."

We knew property values had dropped appreciably. City Slick was impressed with the inside of the pink house, especially the burgundy carpet—just their color—but his offer was much less than my investment. I couldn't accept. Following his offer, I showed the house to several sannyasins. One couple told me they would have bought it, but City Slick advised against it. I told Darleen if the Rajneeshees could not own the pink house, they would have me stay there in order to further endure their intimidations.

About the same time that City Slick was negotiating to buy houses in Antelope, the hierarchy assigned carloads of red-clothed sannyasins to visit small towns in western Oregon and Washington. They were to investigate any large buildings that were for sale and suggest that the Bhagwan was interested in buying them.

They did not want those buildings. It was a ploy. What they really wanted was for the state capital to be deluged with letters from these communities asking the State of Oregon to recognize the city of Rajneeshpuram—give them what they wanted—and keep them "over there".

Finally the state treasurer did send their city revenue-sharing funds from gasoline, liquor and cigarette taxes. From December 1982 to June 1983 they received $10,486.86. On one of my visits to the capital, I found Governor Vic Atiyeh talking with a man in the large reception room, where he held open house sometimes.

When the man came out, I went in. I introduced myself. He smiled. I told him I was from Antelope. His smile disappeared. Just the mention of Antelope to a politician meant trouble! I took a deep breath and then told him exactly what I thought of state funds supporting the closed city built for a religious sect. "Are they still getting that?" he asked of me!

Almost on any given day, Rajneeshees could be seen in the state capital. They lobbied on many issues, and in each case, if they had been successful, their city's status would have been secure.

My fried Raye and I made a trip to the capital to lobby also. A state senate hearing was announced, and the proposed law to be discussed was one in which the Rajneeshees were trying to inject a segment, which, again, would have benefited them.

Senator Kitzhabor was chairman, and when we arrived, I leaned over the desk toward him and asked if we might speak against their proposal. I remember very well the pat he gave the back of my hand as he said, "You will be given time to speak." L. B. Day was on the committee also, and he emphatically told the Rajneeshees that what they were discussing was as logical as comparing apples and oranges. Following the hearing, I sat down next to him, and he said, "You have nothing to worry about." The attitude of these two prestigious members of the Senate allayed our fears, but this helpful attitude came too late for Antelope, where only fifteen of the original forty residents remained.

From July 1983 to July 1987, $118,547.09 was scheduled for Rajneeshpuram; however, these funds were withheld and ultimately distributed to other cities. Attorney General Dave Frohnmayer said, "We believe that drawing money from the state inescapably aids a specific religion." He found the land to be owned by a religious foundation, leased to a religious commune and populated exclusively by followers of the religious leader. The U.S. District Court ruled that Rajneeshpuram was illegal from the date of its attempted incorporation. Rajneeshpuram was defunct!

Six

The first of April I answered the telephone and a young woman said, "I understand you have a lot of new people in town."

"What makes you say that?" I asked.

"My boyfriend and his brother have moved to Antelope. The Bhagwan sent word to the Nirvana center in Seattle that everyone should move there."

Further conversation with Sunny Miller disclosed that her friend was a follower, and she was working diligently to break his tie to the cult, but he quit his job at Boeing Aircraft in order to answer his master's call. She went on to say that if he had known he was moving to Antelope to throw a vote, he might not have been so quick to comply.

We checked the voter registration cards and found that he, Barry Brittain, and his brother Scott Peterson were registered and declared their address as that of the Viola Wilson house. Within two months following the election, both men were back home in Seattle living with their mother.

I met Sunny on election day, when she, as well as others, spent that infamous day in April in the pink house in order to observe the election and its outcome firsthand. She and I kept in touch for several years during which time she married— not to the old friend whom who had tried unsuccessfully to help.

Obviously the Rajneeshees were preparing to move enough people from the ranch to Antelope to insure their numerical superiority at the polls. At this very time statewide papers carried Rajneesh press releases, "No, they did not intend to move people into Antelope to control the election." Almost to the very day that they bought Darleen's house another press release said there was no intention to do anything against the old-timers; even so, in the middle of the night of April fourteenth, more followers were bussed in from the Muddy ranch to occupy a small, retired sheepherder's cottage which they had just purchased over the telephone. So quickly was the transaction made that no key was available. They broke in, in order to sleep there the eve of election.

Rajneeshee voters were neither property owners nor were they renters; furthermore, they registered as many as six and nine in houses where only four adults were considered legal residents by the State Department of Health—a useful fact we failed to use.

Every house in town has its own septic system, and the minimum lot size provides for only a two-bedroom structure. In other words, no more than four permanent residents per house.

On April fifteenth the votes were cast and counted, fifty-five reds voted, no, forty-one unreds voted yes. The charter remained intact and vulnerable to Bhagwan's takeover in the November general election.

The loss of the election to disincorporate was the emotional breaking point to us. I observed personality changes—neighbors quick to quarrel with neighbor and stranger alike. A steady stream of sightseers traveling throughout town asking directions to "that ranch" were often the recipients of rudeness.

My hands shook. I couldn't paint, but I had already stopped sitting on a backroad in that colorful terrain, because I felt a growing fear that I was a likely target for an accident anytime I was by myself in the back country.

Others experienced similar fear. I stopped in Maupin one evening on my way home, and there in the Riverside Hotel I visited with rancher John Conroy. John had been appointed to fill the county vacancy created when the cattle-selling judge left the country on the missionary assignment.

John is Irish with the stature to make a formidable opponent—one not to be antagonized. So when he warned me that I should be very careful driving the lonesome Bakeoven Road after dark, he got my attention. He frightened me even more when he said, "We are both targets. We could be edged off the road into the canyon, and no one would know how we got there!"

When he saw me pale, he added, "Don't worry tonight, Donna, my headlights will be right behind you all the way to my lane." His lane was twelve miles from my home. They were long miles.

As the tranquility of our environment diminished, so did the quality of my marriage, which, from the beginning, was a difficult challenge. From Reno on our belated honeymoon, I called my lawyer and asked him to, "Get me out of this mess." He had met Donald, liked him, and so he told me I had been a hermit too long, that I had to adjust, but I did not care enough.

In the meantime, my neighbor Agnes had been stricken with diabetes which her doctor attributed to stress. She was on the town council just prior to the Rajneeshee takeover, and the council was struggling with their demand for a building permit in order to construct a huge business structure, which, if completed and used, would have jeopardized our water supply.

In poor health, Agnes was forced to move back to the Willamette Valley, and, like Darleen, she will not return to set eyes on her home. Soon after her departure, I made arrangements for Donald to rent her house, and so we became good neighbors—not Mr. and Mrs. I did his laundry. He mowed my lawn.

Throughout the summer of 1982 Rajneesh's free-labor force graded, bladed, filled and chartered new roads on the Muddy. Hundreds of young people worked from dawn to dusk at Bhagwan's behest, so we weren't surprised when the news teams were wondrously impressed with the changes in the sagebrush; however, not one writer noted that the topsoil is very shallow and the vegetation roots tenuous. The heavy equipment dislodging the fragile root system of the nutritional, natural grasses was in fact destructive.

While the public and press were propagandized with statements such as, "reclaiming the rundown ranch, building an oasis in the desert, complete organic farming, (until the weeds prevailed) protection of all wildlife," we saw acres of hillsides eroded, because plows had tilled the natural growth from the soil. They said they were going to riprap the creek banks to hold the soil. We drove through and saw they had cut the pine trees growing along the banks of the creeks and used them for riprap!

It was about this time they advertised worldwide to the followers that anyone sending one hundred dollars to Rajneeshpuram would have a tree planted in the donor's name. Oldtime farmers smiled in the knowledge that before spring the deer would browse those trees to sticks. It was the money, not the trees Rajneesh sought.

Yes, Rajneeshees were farmers—their crop was people, and members of the press were their best recruiters, as they parroted the Rajneeshee plans. Rajneesh loved all publicity whether good or bad in content. It was good for delivering would-be followers to his door.

The gate to Rajneeshpuram was Antelope where we began to lock our doors in fear of the many strange people who came seeking the Bhagwan Shree Rajneesh.

They came, those adventurous, pseudo farmers prepared to give everything they had in order to be a part of this beautiful plan where everyone lived a life-style unfettered by moral codes.

Fathers came with small children. Mothers came without their children. They came in pairs and alone on buses, bikes, cycles and shank's bones. They all came to Antelope to ask directions to "that ranch", and so Antelope was deluged with strangers looking for lodging or transportation to Madras, because, you see, many of these folks who had been lured by enchanting news articles were rejected at the Rajneeshee office in Antelope which served as a screening point for those going to the ranch. Sheela had said soon after their arrival, "I shall decide who comes in, but not who leaves."

One day while I was gone a young man found my outside key and was seen entering my house. A neighbor had already called the sheriff since this stranger had knocked on several doors asking permission to take a shower. When the sheriff detained him, he said he was Jesus Christ, and when the Bhagwan would set eyes upon him, he (Bhagwan) would leave and Antelope would be peaceful again! He was later institutionalized.

Another time our postmaster found a man sleeping in his barn. He gave him ten dollars so he would leave.

Viola Wilson found that someone had been sleeping in the back of her enclosed pickup, and Wheeler Meyer answered his door to meet a father with his young daughter asking for transportation to Madras. They had been rejected as commune members. It was one of Antelope's rare rainy nights. Because my neighbor felt sorry for the child, he drove them the thirty-eight miles to the bus depot, where the stranger paid him with an antique coin for his kindness. When Wheeler asked the would-be Rajneeshee why he wanted to live on the Muddy ranch, he replied that he was just curious—wanted to see what it was like, however, he had left a wife and other children in Klamath Falls in order to satisfy that curiosity!

So the stories grew, as both pauper and elite, came to our town, where skilled Rajneeshees appraised their worth and ability to contribute to the Bhagwan. Acceptance or rejection was determined by their value.

Even the Rajneeshees called the county sheriff to eject a wayfarer who slept in his bedroll in the park. He had insisted on visiting with Bhagwan and refused to leave until he did. Bhagwan was what an insurance salesman might call an "attractive nuisance."

But the sannyasins who were assigned short visits to Antelope from the ranch posed no threat, and no particular one was seen in town very long. We decided their stay in Antelope was tantamount to the armed services Rest and Relaxation.

I purposefully engaged them in mundane conversation whenever possible. It was one way to learn something of these people, besides I was curious and wanted to discover some shared characteristics of these followers who gave up everything to be in the presence of a living master who in return demanded from them complete submission. Many were glassy-eyed and some had difficulty conversing.

One winter evening on my way to visit Annie, I encountered a follower standing in a hole he was digging. The wind was blowing fiercely, and he was bareheaded. I asked him where his hat was. His eyes got wide, and he slowly answered, "I had one, but I broke it."

Soon after they purchased the Antelope cafe, but they had not yet taken occupancy, I found two followers with a long measuring tape measuring the width of lots on Main Street. When they entered the cafe, I followed. They proceeded to measure the depth of the rooms and width of the doors, but never did they write down their findings!

A newswriter stopped into the pink house after visiting the Muddy and said he had followed the suggestion to break away from the tour guide and question laborers. He asked several questions of one sannyasin and received answers which he guessed were Hindu proverbs!

It is difficult to understand a cult leader's control over his subject's thinking; however, a resident of India who knew of the Bhagwan in his native land came to visit Rajneeshpuram and told the Bend Bulletin; "Because Americans are less sophisticated than Indians about methods of mind control, Americans can be victimized by Indians. Americans traditionally have had little belief in and exposure to the effects of mesmerism and hypnotism and trances—and hence have few defenses against their practitioners."

Working twelve hours every day, deprived of proper diet, and sleeping in buildings without running water resulted in followers becoming disenchanted with the place that boasted free sex as a major asset. As one ex-follower said, "Who cares about sex after laboring all day everyday?"

So how does one leave? The nearest bus station is over sixty miles away, and drivers on the lonely roads to that bus station were not apt to give a ride to anyone dressed in red.

Perhaps the greatest obstacle to leaving was the lack of money. The Bhagwan got the money. Maybe a letter to Mom to come and pick up her child was one way to escape, but all mail leaving the Rajneeshpuram post office was censored! Would Mom have gotten the letter?

A Rajneeshpuram interoffice memorandum stated, "no sealed envelopes would leave the post office." John Silvertooth-Stewart found it and other documents from the Rajneesh office in the Antelope city dump, because some worker had failed to put them through the paper shredder. He gave the memo to Portland television station KOIN.

A panel of three from the station, headed by Peter Murphy, held a live telecast with Ma Anand Sheela who was always eager to be seen on the airwaves. The contents of the purloined memo were brought to her attention. "I don't read memos," she parried the accusation of censorship, but thrown off guard, she unwittingly admitted that envelopes had to be left unsealed until they reached a special room where they were sealed and then mailed. She insisted that that was the most expeditious method; furthermore, she volunteered that all incoming mail was opened before delivery in order to stop any possible drug trafficking. Thus, complete censorship of mail existed at Rajneeshpuram.

Bhagwan attracted so many people, he could be eclectic in his selection of followers. He was proud to publicize the many college graduates and master's degrees found among his devotees, but most of his intellectuals were assigned duties foreign to their education. A math major from Wisconsin was the cook at the cafe. A schoolteacher from Missouri was housecleaner for the nine corporate-owned houses in Antelope, and a physician from California was driving nails as a carpenter. "Cleaning a floor can be a tremendously creative act," so says Bhagwan, most convincingly.

One major step toward attaining enlightenment is the destruction of the ego, so the master separates many of his followers from their skills and accomplishments, and he assigns them meaningless tasks, but that is only one of the salmagundi tactics Bhagwan applied to create the "mindless, egoless man."

From the beginning of his self-appointed godship in India, Bhagwan had sponsored, for a price, dynamic therapy classes where the participants were encouraged to act out their sexual fantasies and frustrations. Broken bones, rapes and mental disorientation were the results.

When one sannyasin questioned the master as to the merits of the beatings, Bhagwan answered, "None of your business." The particular therapy leader from Poona, India who encouraged the violence moved to Rajneeshpuram, but when the hierarchy was questioned about the continuation of these violent activities, they scoffed and said they no longer held such classes. Their act had been cleaned up, they said.

Cult leaders inherently say one thing while their deeds exhibit the diverse.

A local doctor told me he had set many broken bones for Rajneeshees when they first arrived. He was told the fractures were the result of farm accidents. Soon the Muddy Ranch had its own doctors in residence to care for the followers.

The nucleus of the power in Oregon was the same that had oiled the machine in Poona, India. How could we believe their therapy classes were less violent?

SEVEN

The Antelope Cafe had been for sale before the Rajneesh arrived. The proprietor would whimsically place a For Sale sign in the window and remove it depending upon her health and attitude. Rajneesh bought the cafe at a price that would have built a new structure on their commercial property, but they knew the hub of the valley was that cafe where, throughout everyday, almost everyone visited to exchange the daily news, read the newsy bulletin board, discuss ranch operations and pick up the mail next door.

None of the children attending the Antelope school lived in town. They came from outlying ranches, and parents who came to take their children home would often stop at the cafe; also, the post office served these outlying ranchers. So you see the cafe and the attached post office were visited regularly by numerous folks from miles around. Once the Rajneeshees became evident in town, they were the number one conversational topic.

The loss of that cafe was a severe blow to the integrity of the valley. We were teary-eyed when sannyasins removed its sign—a likeness of an antelope, and in its place hung a large red banner with two doves in flight. They renamed it Zorba de Buddha. The two doves embraced all the Bhagwan's writings, and that symbol of Rajneeshism was later adopted by the Rajneesh-controlled government as the city seal!

In July of 1982 the Rajneeshees held their first "Celebration of the Moon" which included an esoteric day in order for followers to pay homage to the master. Advertisements were sent worldwide which later brought an attendance of over six thousand. Those arriving by bus made a mandatory stop at their cafe in Antelope where a boutique had been added—another money-making scheme.

We saw the entire celebration as a money-making effort. One week's lodging was $350.00, and numerous classes in meditation and psychological therapy were offered for addi-

RAJNEESH INTERNATIONAL MEDITATION UNIVERSITY

- P.O. Box 5, Rajneeshpuram, OR 97741 USA, Tel: (503) 489-3328

COURSES

Rajneesh Breath Therapy Course

Mar 23 - Apr 26	$2500**
Jul 12 - Aug 15	$2500**

Rajneesh Breath Therapy is a breathing technique which opens up and releases energy held in the body. This course can be taken for personal transformation and as training for giving sessions in Rajneesh Breath Therapy.

Coordinated by: **Ma Deva Gambhira,** M.M., D.M.(RIMU), Siddha

Rajneesh Rebalancing Course

Mar 7 - Jun 19	$7500**
Jul 12 - Oct 24	$7500**
Nov 14 - Feb 26	$7500**

With Bhagwan's vision of the total man, this course teaches you body awareness, how to get in tune with your energy, open up and relax, and how to help others make the same discovery. The first aspect deals with the theory and anatomy of rebalancing, including practical experience in breath release and spinal balancing skills, as well as methods of joint mobilization and deep connective tissue manipulation. The second aspect focuses on energy work–the application of Rajneesh bodywork techniques

developed to transform the body and its energy.

Coordinated by: **Swami Prem Anubuddha,** M.M., D.M.(RIMU), Siddha
                 Swami Prem Satyarthi, M.M., D.M.(RIMU), Arihanta

Rajneesh DeHypnotherapy Basic Course

Mar 22 - Jun 19	$5500**
Jul 13 - Oct 12	$5500**

Rajneesh DeHypnotherapy is a soft and powerful process of separating reality from unreality. Participants learn that only the here and now is real. It is a highly practical and effective program which opens the pathway to higher consciousness and, at the same time, makes everyday life simpler and easier. The course itself is not a training program but can be taken separately as an extended workshop.

Coordinated by: **Swami Anand Santosh,** M.M., D.Litt.M.(RIMU), Siddha

*"Rajneesh" is a trademark owned by Rajneesh Foundation International.

**This price includes accommodations and three vegetarian meals per day, which are furnished by Rajneesh Neo-Sannyas International Commune subject to the conditions set out in the course registration.

This advertisement, circulated worldwide in the Rajneesh Times, is an example of the prices charged and classes offered at Rajneeshpuram.

tional fees, plus, all guests were encouraged to participate in the "growth" of the commune by working at designated tasks.

The Oregon Revised Statutes clearly state that mass gathering permits must be obtained before any advertising may be done. Before Wasco and Jefferson County had granted the permit, the Rajneeshees advertised worldwide the event. From the back room of their cafe, I found a paper carrying the lengthy ad. When I advised the Wasco County district attorney, he asked me to testify before a grand jury. I did. Nothing happened.

That same day Sheela's husband, John Shelfer a.k.a. Jayananda, accompanied by a local attorney testified before the grand jury. A witness before a grand jury is not permitted to have an attorney present. Again, nothing happened.

Donald came home from the post office one day during the celebration with a particularly sad observation. "Many beautiful young women are arriving and will soon be ushered to the ranch to participate in new and unknown experiences."

The post office was under the same roof as the cafe, and whoever owned the cafe (now the Rajneesh) received a governmental rental check for housing it. The Rajneeshees made several complaints about the local postmaster, Bill Dickson (the John Wayne look-a-like) to the postmaster general in Portland, and one night on live television they falsely accused him of opening a letter. Of course they wanted to replace him with a sannyasin and collect the postmaster's salary for the Bhagwan, too. And how secure would our mail be in their hands?

Not long after they moved into their cafe, the local men began meeting at Al's Antelope Garage, another vintage building that had been an actual thriving business in Antelope's past. It is on Main Street and anyone seeing Al Kuhlman's truck there and the door open felt welcome to step in and commiserate.

The Rajneeshees accused the fellows of holding clandestine city meetings there and took photographs of those who came and left.

Constant surveillance of all our actions seemed their daily mission.

Because no visible help was coming to our aid, I felt compelled to do something other than writing letters and calling unresponsive bureaucrats, so I contacted the Rotary club in Redmond to ask if they wanted to hear some of the real stuff that was happening to Antelopeans. That speech led to others.

Central and north central Oregon were better advised as to the inroads Bhagwan was making due to the superior newspaper coverage delivered by the Bend Bulletin and The Dalles Reminder. In the densely populated Willamette Valley the Willamette Weekly in three editions carried factual information as well as Oregon Magazine whose writer Win McCormack did noteworthy investigative reporting. Oregon's largest newspaper, the Oregonian, favored press releases from the public relations staff of the Bhagwan until 1985 when it was apparent the Rajneeshees had lost their battle to establish a separate state within our state.

Donald went with me to that first rotary meeting. I was concerned, because I was not nervous. "That's because you're prepared," he said. Public opinion was another avenue wherein we could gain strength for our cause. We needed more public outcry for the expeditious deportation of Bhagwan, and I calmly set out to collect all the public opinion I could.

My speeches were from notes only, with each one different due to up-to-date information added as the confrontation unfolded; however, background data remained the same, i.e. the Bhagwan had held classes in which women were raped, bones broken and minds destroyed. He held classes in which he advised pregnant women to have abortions in order to "save your energy for yourself." In his clinic in Poona, young women submitted to sterilization in order to prove their allegiance. Janet Stewart accompanied me on these speaking engagements lending much support.

Following such an expose´, I would conclude with a famous quote from Edmund Burke, "The only way for evil to flourish is for good men to do nothing." Many listeners were moved to ask what they could do to help, and my answer was to send money to the 1,000 Friends of Oregon who were opposing the colonization of the farmland in the courts and to write to their congressmen and call the immigration office to request fast investigation into Bhagwan's visa.

Fighting for Antelope's freedom and trying to adjust to the problems in my personal life placed untold stress upon me.

I finally filed for the divorce I knew was necessary and sold my pink house to a young man who fell in love with it just as I had, but before I moved back to the Willamette Valley, I had made friends of a telephone pal, Mrs. Inez Hartung. She called me frequently for Bhagwan reports, and was a true champion of Antelope, probably because she owned a ranch on the Deschutes River not too many miles away.

Though we had not met personally, when she found out that I was getting on-the-job training as a public speaker, she began seeking engagements for me. The first one was in May 1982 at the Portland City Club.

When attorney Garry McMurry learned of the opening held for me, he chose to speak in my place. He did not believe I could handle such a prestigious audience, but I believe anyone saturated with a particular subject from a firsthand accounting who is willing to discuss that subject is a real candidate for oratory.

A lawyer asked me one day why I did those things (wrote letters and made speeches) which would precipitate a lawsuit, I answered I did not know. I did know the public response that followed each speech made me feel ten feet tall. I was helping Antelope.

Perhaps an astrologer would say I orated because I am a Gemini born with Mercury the messenger my ruling planet. A numerologist might say it may be because I am a "three" and three governs expression and communication. For whatever reason, I was determined to disseminate the facts surrounding the Bhagwan's cult.

In order to keep up-to-date on the new government in Antelope after I moved, I drove over the mountain the first Tuesday of every month to observe the Rajneeshee council in action. On that council sat Janet's son, John Silvertooth-Stewart. He ran for that post in the general election of November 1982, and with the preponderance of Rajneeshee voters, it was a surprise to us that he garnered 96 votes. Leo Butcher got 89 votes, and Verne Mobley, who was not even in the race, got 69 write-in votes. The Rajneeshee public relations staff must have determined the voting; after all, the entire world was watching the outcome.

John Silvertooth-Stewart

Leo would not serve, and Verne never intended to be a candidate, and so John was the only non-Rajneeshee on the council. A juxtaposition not to be envied. Some of the old-timers looked askance at his assumed roll, but I knew the impetus behind his actions and defended him when necessary.

His moxie and intellect saw him through one year of the sham. Finally, he tendered his resignation and moved to Eugene. He wrote to his friend Wil Phinney at The Dalles Reminder, gave him his new address and told him of his resignation. The letter inadvertently was published in the Letters to the Editor column. In it John had written, "I want to be pretty quiet especially so that the orange people don't find me." In order to protect him from "an unpleasant encounter with Rajneeshees" another letter was quickly published, the tenor of which protected him. Here are a couple of excerpts.

I am getting out of the pressure cooker. I'm just burned out on the whole thing. As I stated to you often, I always was hopeful that things could work out and the tensions would ease eventually and everyone could live under the sun.

However, things just keep on keeping on and there is less and less middle ground to stand on. I am telling everyone to hang in there . . . the government moves so slow—myriad of local, state and federal agencies all trying to respond to complex issues and political pressures—two groups of people poles apart in various stages of culture shock . . .

It used to be that Antelope was in the far end of the world. Now it is like a big fish bowl in the middle of an international zoo. I'm tired of being one of the oddities on display.

I begged Portland-based television stations to visit those meetings and document the unique political activities. David Cash of the Bend Bulletin and Will Phinney of The Dalles Reminder came regularly, and so some newspaper coverage existed. Antelope resident Mrs. Jean Opray taped them—an act that would later cause her and her husband considerable grief.

Meetings were held in the basement of the school. The conference table was covered with a red cloth, and the meetings began and ended with a joke. One of the first ordinances passed was that all residents should, "live, love and laugh." There were other frivolous ordinances.

Ordinance #62 ordained: "Block 5, Bairds Addition, Antelope, will be set aside as a place where citizens and visitors to Antelope may gather without wearing clothing, and relax with each other in true openness and honesty. This ordinance shall take effect after proper facilities, as determined by the Council, have been provided, and the Council announces the park opening. Passed June 7, 1983."

I don't know what "proper facilities" entailed, but I do know that the lot mentioned was a dry weedy patch of hillside just west of town proper. That lot was never developed in any way, and their ordinance was probably just another tack to harass the remaining old-timers; after all, they had 64,000 acres upon which to romp and roam completely unobserved.

The council adopted the Bhagwan's religious emblem of two doves in flight, one representing the master and one representing the follower, as the city seal. All his materials bore that symbol. Where was the separation of church and state?

They passed three ordinances to hire Rajneeshee personnel from Rajneeshpuram to engage in work for the city of Antelope. They hired that city's attorney at $100.00 an hour to attend the Antelope council meetings, and so I wrote to the Oregon State Ethics Commission and suggested there existed a conflict of interest, inasmuch as these people all relied upon the commune for their every sustenance. That commission began an investigation, but before they arrived at a decision, they said they ran out of funds to investigate further!

When the Rajneesh council learned that I had advised that state bureau of their possible conflict of interest, they then—after the fact—ran advertisements for bids for those three particular jobs. Of course, the bids from Rajneeshpuram were the lowest.

This new government found many ways to increase the city's expenses in order to justify the city budget—a budget which in its first year was second to Eugene, Oregon, and the second year ranked first with the highest taxes in the entire state!

Donald attended their first three city meetings, but he could not cope with the pseudo government. He drank before going and defied their No Smoking edict. Soon a county sheriff was necessary to assure orderly conduct. Donald was served with a lawsuit following one meeting in which he grabbed a Swami's shirt sleeve in order to detain him so he would be forced to listen to his version of a contested issue. The suit alleged he picked up the young man, assaulted him and caused him such distress that he vomited for three days and required the constant care of a psychiatrist due to fright!

We all laughed at that ridiculous charge. There were enough of us old-timers there to refute that charge, but it made a good story to fuel the fires of propaganda on the ranch where followers were told how dangerous *we* were to *them*. Cults use any opportunity to cement an "Us Versus Them" atmosphere. It is appropriate to state here that commune members had no access to outside information through newspapers and television sets.

.

EIGHT

Sheela solicited an interview with Merv Griffin on nationwide television, and Rosemary McGreer of Clarno agreed to represent Antelope. Because Rosemary had the courage to state some facts about Bhagwan and his commune, she was promptly sued for over two million dollars. Before Bhagwan's attorney filed the suit, she was given the opportunity of retracting her statements, but had the character and courage not to do so. She made three comments not to Bhagwan's liking; one, the hierarchy lived in a life-style quite different from the followers who worked twelve hours a day with only sustenance for pay; two, the children were housed in a dormitory separate from parents, and three, they claimed to be farmers, but were building a city. All facts.

Rosemary is not a resident of the city of Antelope, but lives on the John Day River at Clarno on a ranch with her husband Kelly and their two children. Kelly is the fourth generation of McGreers to farm the land so their interest in what was happening across the fence from them was more than simple concern.

Rosemary counterfiled with a lawsuit claiming defamation based on a letter written by Sheela and printed in the Rajneesh Times. Here is Sheela's letter:

Beloved Friend, Love. The Rajneesh community in Oregon has been the object of many threats during the past few months. A relatively small number of people who are themselves no better than thugs have been trying to scare us out of the state by threatening the lives of Rajneeshees, or those of our friends, or trying to destroy our property.

Cowardly, inhuman acts such as the recent maiming of a horse owned by Harry Hawkins, the Rajneeshpuram Peace Officer who served as a deputy sheriff in Jefferson County for five years, are typical of the kind of people involved.

We are tired of this uncivilized, barbaric unsophisticated and violent way of trying to intimidate the religious minority.

Once and for all, we wish to make it clear that we are here in Oregon to stay at whatever the cost.

If that means that some of our blood is spilled, or some of our property vandalized, then that is the price we are prepared to pay. The only effect of such actions will be to increase public support and understanding for us.

Rosemary McGreer, Donna Smith Quick, Robert Anderson, Diane McDonald, Bill Driver, Wil Phinney, Don Smith, Loren Reynolds, Mardo Jiminez, Barbara Hill and all of those insolent racists and religious bigots who go around the state—supported by Senator Mark Hatfield and a few government bureaucrats—spreading fear through outrageous lies and biased opinions should understand one thing; this atmosphere of violence and threats is your offspring.

For our part, we will not hesitate to pursue every legal means to defend ourselves, making full use of the protection offered by American justice and the Constitution. We have a growing staff of highly qualified attorneys to defend our rights and the financial resources to fight any court case to the highest levels of appeal.

Rosemary's defense attorney, Carrell F. Bradley, made a presentation at a summary judgment hearing, prior to trial date, that left little room for argument. Multnomah County Judge, Clifford B. Olson, dismissed the Rajneesh case against her stating, "This is a tempest in a teapot." later he awarded her damages in the amount of $75,000.

After Rosemary's appearance on the Merv Griffin show, I was invited to confront Sheela on statewide television, a program "Between the Lines" on KGW. The telecast was Sunday, May 1, 1983. Sheela was to remain at the ranch and be seen with Robert Anderson, a defector, and me via remote control. Friday before the airing, the moderator, Jim Althoff, called to advise me that instead of Sheela from the ranch, they were flying in the then-mayor of Rajneeshpuram, City Slick.

I wanted to cancel my appearance right then. Why was he replacing Sheela? I had considered him the "big gun" and Sheela no challenge as a debater. Who was he after, the defector or me?

Sunday afternoon I left home with courageous thoughts of maintaining a relaxed demeanor regardless of what might befall. I certainly needed all the strength and moral support I could muster. Again, Janet went with me. We arrived early as did Robert Anderson. When Dave Knapp (City Slick) arrived, the moderator ushered him out of sight. I told Robert, "Let's go find those two," but we were intercepted by the program manager who told us we had no business wandering around.

Airtime arrived. Immediately following the opening introduction, Dave Knapp handed me papers announcing they were a suit claiming defamation. He turned to Robert and said, "Sorry I don't have any for you. In time they may come." The papers were bogus. The legal ones arrived twenty days later asking $990,000 in damages.

His opening remarks were intimidating, and were meant to discourage any further opposition. He clearly stated for all the state to hear that Rajneeshees intended to use the court system to quell others such as I.

Robert called me the next day to say he was certain the whole thing had been a setup, and an employee of the station has since agreed. Robert disappeared following that Sunday experience, no doubt due to City Slick's threat to provide him with his own lawsuit at a later date.

Also, the next day the Oregonian carried a news item stating that the charges against me were the result of my remark that Rajneeshees should be slaughtered. How ridiculous! I called the Associated Press writer and inquired where she got such nonsense. "From the mayor of Rajneeshpuram. You know," she continued, "the A.P. has a record of 98% accuracy." "Well, you will surely lose that record if you continue to accept releases from the Bhagwan's people," I returned. She wrote a splendid retraction which included, "Quick abhors violence of any kind." The Bend Bulletin carried it just as it was released over the wire service, but the Oregonian rewrote it leaving me still the author of those ugly words. The basis of the "slaughter" statement was a portion of a letter I sent to the editor of the Valley Times of Tigard.

Five Rajneeshees had held an assembly at the Tigard High School—a proselytizing campaign—which resulted in some irate parents. When Sheela heard of their vehement opposition to Rajneeshees speaking in a public school, she railed against them in an article in the Rajneesh Times. I took that article to the editor who then asked me to write an editorial. Here is my letter:

The master is an expert in propaganda!

Cults exist for only one purpose—the enrichment of a few at the physical and mental expense of many. It is perilous to expose anyone to the rhetoric of their public relations experts, whose delivery obscures the truth.

Those responsible for allowing Ma Anand Sheela an audience at the Tigard High School are highly uninformed. The Rajneesh Times of February 4th quotes Sheela as saying that the parents of students of Tigard High School are unintelligent. She had said many months ago that the citizens of Antelope were ignorant and stupid. Apparently, anyone opposing the Rajneesh is lacking in grey matter.

The Rajneesh Times is, in my opinion, a propaganda sheet for followers, and such a statement regarding the disgruntled parents is not surprising since the cult's first endeavor is the severance of ties between follower and family. The Rajneesh has said, "The single greatest obstacle to human progress is the family unit."

He came to Antelope claiming to be the head of a farming commune when, in fact, he intended at the onset to build a city. He had been looking for a long time for just such a place to build a "city to provoke God." India refused him two plots, because the land was zoned agricultural. It is ironic that we have allowed this Indian outcast to usurp sixty-four thousand acres in Oregon—land zoned "Essential Farm Use." The Oregon Revised Statutes provide for protection of agricultural land. Where are the keepers of the laws?

Too few people have agonized. Too few people have writ-

ten public officials requesting the departure of Rajneesh, posthaste. Too few people care that every taxpayer will be supporting a closed city, a totalitarian state ruled by a master whose every command is obeyed, whether it be "to kill themselves or others, if he asks."

A citizen of Bombay, India, wrote, "They are psychopathic megalomaniacs. You, as Americans, naturally, think you can defeat them by the legal process. You are mistaken. The only way to defeat these criminals is by dirty tactics, the same methods they use themselves. Don't entertain any scruples. If necessary, 'slaughter them,' because, if not, they'll do the same to you when they achieve power."

Those who would live in a controlled environment, i.e. be told what to wear, where to sleep, when and what to eat, and on what to labor should follow a different leader—Uncle Sam. Wear khaki green or sea blue, smile a patriotic smile, maintain their dignity and their right to self-determination, plus collect a salary for their efforts.

Until all property is equally taxed, regardless of its use, cult leaders will grow fat, followers will grow lean, and those working in the free society will support them all.

The master is an expert at propaganda!

The citizen of Bombay had sent the "slaughter" letter to our mayor as a warning. It included suggestions. Here is his complete letter:

I am sorry that I didn't warn you three months ago about these Rajneesh psychopaths, but frankly I was afraid they might find some way to trace me, and take avenge. These characters are psychopathic megalomaniacs, as I've seen from their behavior in Poona.

You as Americans naturally think you can defeat them by due legal process such as transferring jurisdiction of your township to your country or state. You are mistaken. The only way to defeat these criminals is by dirty tactics—the same methods they use themselves. Don't entertain any scruples. If necessary, 'slaughter them,' because if not, they'll do the same to you when they achieve power.

Call in the FBI and the CIA, department D. Try to drive them out, not only out of your area, but out of the USA, and, if possible, out of existence!

Believe me I have seen them here, at first hand. If you delay, it will be too late. Better they should go the way of the Jonesville cyanide suicides, but don't bank on that. They are not losers, they are worthless winners. It is you or them. I hope it will be you.

The erroneous article in the <u>Oregonian</u> distressed me more than the Rajneesh lawsuit for $990,000, and I knew I was in deep trouble. A scholarly friend recommended to me a lawyer who was eager to sue the <u>Oregonian</u>, but Laura Bentley of The Dalles called me twice and told me Garry McMurry, the cult fighter, wished to see me, and so I visited him in order to file a suit against the paper and answer the Rajneeshee complaint. "My friends will think I have slipped over the edge when they read that I want people slaughtered." I wanted to defend myself against those charges first, but Mr. McMurry dissuaded me. He agreed to get a retraction printed. (He never did.) He was extremely enthusiastic to have a case against the Rajneeshees. On July 22, 1983 I recited to members of the media the following press release:

On April 25, 1983 Sheela Silverman in a letter to the Rajneesh Times accused me of threatening violence against the Rajneesh organizations and accused me and others of being insolent racist and religious bigots—"spreading fear through outrageous lies and biased opinions . . . " Sheela also stated, "For our part, we will not hesitate to pursue every legal means to defend ourselves, making full use of the protection offered Americans in American justice and the Constitution. We have a growing staff of highly qualified attorneys to defend our rights and the financial resources to fight any court case to the highest levels of appeal." Ma Anand Sheela made good her threats two days later, May 1st, at 5 p.m. on a television program beamed throughout Oregon, David Knapp handed legal papers to me saying it was a Complaint and that I had been sued. It was a bogus complaint, and was later served upon me alleging defamation.

Despite being sued for $990,000.00, I have not been intimidated into silence from expressing my opinions. My purpose in speaking out about the facts surrounding the Rajneesh organizations is to warn my fellow Oregonians of the dangers inherent in their deeds as compared to their stated purposes and to warn everyone of the threatening effect this group has on our rights to free speech. Today, July 22nd, I have filed a Defamation Action against the Rajneesh organization, Ma Anand Sheela and the Bhagwan Shree Rajneesh for $1,000,000.00 in protection of my rights to discuss the facts surrounding the Rajneesh.

I also want my friends and neighbors to be aware that our right to free speech guaranteed by the Constitutions of the U.S. and Oregon, our right to freely discuss our opinions without fear of reprisal is at risk in this state. I hope to prove that the right of free speech still exists for all of us. Thank you.

I knew nothing of the ramifications of filing a lawsuit, but Rosemary had already been successful with the infamous letter written by Sheela, and Mr. McMurry was complacent. He agreed not to charge me for his services, and he was certain we would win, and so I had nothing to lose—I thought.

To gain public sympathy, the Rajneesh's public relations force began to use the media to publicize their fears of violence, a tactic they employed in Poona whenever they needed allies. We were all exposed to their daily reports of threats, and sure enough within weeks three bombs exploded on the second floor of the Rajneesh Hotel in Portland. Two days after that bombing two of the hierarchy, Ma Prem Isabel on local radio, and City Slick on television, stated I, by name, and others like me had created the atmosphere that resulted in the blast. My immediate reaction to those lies was one of fear— fear for my safety.

The Bhagwan had many dedicated followers in the Portland area. I felt one of them might, if still able to function, seek me out in order to do the master a favor.

I called Mr. McMurry's home the evening of their last accusing remark and left a message on his answering service. "You've got to do something to stop these false accusations against me before some sannyasin does me in. I'm scared!"

An interesting note here is that while in Poona two firebombs were exploded within the ashram, burning the library which had housed the Bhagwan's many books. The inspector general determined that no Poonite had cast the bombs, but someone had from within the ashram. The Rajneeshees filed an insurance claim for the loss of the books, but collected nothing. The insurance company found that those books were in transit to the U.S. at the time of the fire!

By now the immigration department was receiving much mail asking for the swift deportation of the Indian guru, and I took some credit for many of the letters.

I made frequent trips to the immigration office in Portland to ask about their progress. On one of these trips the head official, Mr. Krueger (now retired) carried into Mr. Hunter's office a large armload of unopened letters all relevant to Bhagwan's deportation. At the same time he pointed out the many cardboard boxes stacked against the wall. "All full and brought in by the Rajneeshees—information supporting his status as a religious teacher. All that has to be handled."

"We'll have to go to Washington and get you some help," I said in jest, but those words in *jest* took root in *fact* when I mentioned the conversation to my friend JoAnne Boies of Albany. She had been writing letters, calling congressmen and visiting the state capital in her many efforts to liberate Antelope.

She called Congressman Jim Weaver, and through his office in Washington D.C. an itinerary was arranged. She not only worked out the details with his office, she collected sufficient funds to pay my expenses and, again, my right arm, Janet said she would go, too. She knew I would not have gone without her. Antelope, her birthplace, meant more to her than anyone else in this fray.

We left on August 10, 1983 to carry the Bhagwan story to

all the governmental bureaus. We were accorded great courtesy (two little old ladies from Antelope) and ample time to speak of the plight of our town and Oregon. In some of the offices a full committee took notes on our delivery. We took pertinent information to all bureaus relevant to their duties, and when we left, we left behind corroborating literature and always made a strong plea for assistance for the Portland offices of INS.

Following that visit considerable pressure was put on the local office to expedite their investigation. Ultimately, it was the Federal Immigration and Naturalization Bureau that pulled the cornerstone out from under the Bhagwan's empire and caused it to crumble; however, I expect some state politicians, to further their political careers, would be taking credit for their after-the-fact aid, and they have done just that—used the Antelope issue as a stepping stone to greater political fame.

Some of us Antelopeans along with her friends throughout the state know that the many elected officials and state bureaucrats who received letters from us failed to respond for over eighteen months, and when some of these people finally took issue with Rajneesh, it was the result of considerable prodding. You could say they were nagged into action.

From personal observations of governmental employees, I have found some must have a carrot dangled before them or a prickly prod used behind them before they will exercise the power of their office.

Six weeks after we returned from Washington, Janet and I made another visit to Mr. Hunter's office, and he told us an additional clerk and an investigator had been on duty for three weeks. "Unheard of in civil service. Under normal circumstances, it takes about three months for the body to arrive."

Mission accomplished.

NINE

After I moved from Antelope back to the Willamette Valley, Inez Hartung made arrangements for me to speak to the Beaverton Rotary Club, and that lead to other speaking engagements. Many times I was asked to give the "other side" of a debate after Rajneeshees had spoken, but when teachers in the Portland school district asked me to give the Antelope story, I decided to end all such debates.

I am adamant that no cult member should be given time and platform in a public school—a desirable place to recruit— so I sought to speak before the leaders of the parent-teacher's organization of Portland Public Schools District Number One. The outcome was the most gratifying of all my efforts. They adopted a rule that cult members will not be permitted a school platform. Wonderful!

Soon the Bhagwan recognized a formidable opponent, one to be muzzled. In March of 1983 word reached me that Sunshine, a Rajneeshpuram "Twinkie" hostess, said steps would have to be taken to shut me up. The lawsuit filed against me was no surprise: however, I still would not be daunted by them into silence.

I had learned early from rancher Jon Bowerman of Clarno, who lives on a ranch across the John Day River from the Muddy, to sit right next to their hierarchy in the front row, look them in the eyes, extend a cheerful greeting and *never* acquiesce.

Jon often spoke at public meetings even during his busy harvest season when he arrived in dusty jeans, boots, and a well-shaped and worn western hat. He was a welcome sight at meetings and also at the front door of the pink house. He spoke in a downhome fashion with great clarity as he challenged Rajneeshee plans. By appearance he is a hero directly from the pages of a Zane Grey novel. Underneath his benign exterior is a supreme intellect with a sense of humor that he lavishly used to cheer many of us through disheartening periods.

The following is the first of many satirical articles he took time from ranch chores to write. His subsequent articles appeared in the Madras and Condon papers which undoubtedly increased their circulation. Here is the first one:

Several ranchers stood in front of the Clarno Grange last December discussing prospects for the coming year. Cattle and hay prices were down and wheat was nothing to brag on. One rancher was more worried than the rest. He didn't think he could get the bank to ride with him for another year.

A neighbor suggested that he set himself up as a nonprofit organization. His reply was simple: "I've been nonprofit for the past ten years, but I still pay my property taxes."

Several of the group could trace their roots back more than 100 years in the area. They had served the community and helped their neighbors, paid their taxes and served in the armed forces. They had buried less fortunate companions in the sands of Normandy and Iwo Jima, the frozen mud in Korea and the jungles of Vietnam.

Now they felt frustrated that foreign money could purchase the legal machinery to obtain special privileges from the government that they themselves could not. "Why can't we?" someone asked. A lively discussion followed and it was agreed it could be done. The group moved inside the grange hall to make a master plan.

It was dark, but they couldn't turn on the lights. The boys from the Wasco Electric Co-op had been putting most of their time in on the Muddy Ranch putting in new power lines. You couldn't blame the co-op. The new owners of the Muddy paid cash while many of the old time farmers and ranchers sometimes didn't have the cash to pay on time.

They lit a candle and in the light of that candle the Church of the Descendants of Oregon Pioneers was born. In that meeting and the ones that followed the plan was mapped out.

The church would be nondenominational and open to any descendant of a pioneer in Wasco, Jefferson or Wheeler counties, or anyone engaged in agriculture in one of those counties for ten years or more.

Since Herb McKay qualified under both provisions, he was considered to be "double registered" and therefore elected leader of the church with the title of Guru.

A law firm was engaged to apply for tax exempt status for all real property and income for the church and its members. Since only a few hundred people and probably not more than 100,000 acres would be involved, it is not anticipated that this will place an undue burden on other residents when they have to assume church member's share of county, state and federal taxes.

The law firm will also petition the 1,000 Friends of Oregon, the Land Conservation and Development Commission and the Wheeler County Planning Commission for the right to establish a town on 1,400 acres presently owned by Huck Rolfe in Eagle Canyon, in Wheeler County. The proposed townsite is most easily reached by riding a horse up the Cottonwood Creek Road and then cutting Charlie Connely's fence. The land is not used for agriculture, although wild horses and Bill Cross' cows sometimes graze the area. It is considered an ideal townsite, because of its inaccessibility.

The town will house a school, veterinary clinic and what is undoubtedly the finest seven volume library in the world today, consisting of the books; "Looking Out for Number One," a volume by Ralph Nader, "Selected Reprints," by syndicated columnist Jack Anderson and four western novels by Louis L'Amour, one of which is written in Japanese.

Members will be requested, but not required, to wear green uniforms, symbolic of the State of Oregon and the Irish ancestry of one of the church founders. (Kelly McGreer) Members with leanings toward Oregon State University or other allergies may wear black or orange with special permission from the guru.

Those who represent the Church of the Descendants of Oregon Pioneers expect wholehearted endorsement of our proposal by everyone in the state. The special privileges *granted to the church members will benefit members and nonmembers alike, particularly county assessors whose work load will be lessened considerably. Signed Jon Bowerman.*

Jon's letters to the editor gave us the ability to find a thread of amusement woven into our sackcloth of despair. Soon everyone was wearing a lapel button upon which was printed a likeness of Herb McKay, the guru, and the words "Descendant of Oregon Pioneer." Just as the Bhagwan's followers wore a mala around their necks, so did Jon. His was made of spent rifle cartridges.

Numerous letters to the editor were printed in the local papers, letters sent by Rajneeshees and non-Rajneeshees. The salutation of all Rajneeshee letters was "Beloved." They ended, "His Blessings." Much contradiction could be found between the "Beloved" and the rhetoric that followed. In the same spirit I wrote the following letter in support of rancher Dave Dickson who had been the recipient of Rajneeshee barbs.

Okay folks, beloved all, settle yourself down for a spell and cast your peepers on a few of the real for sure facts as has befallen us'n over here in Antelope whereupon the remnants of old board walks, the pointed-toed boots of the hard workin', hard ridin', honest to goodness word keepin', tobacco spittin', barn raisin', apple pie eatin', mother lovin' gentry tromp, in minority as it be of today.

Us'n has got these good, loving neighbors sleepin' by the sixes and eights in two bedroom and less houses, moved in so's to vote. They's one little woman doing all that red wash for that parcel of people. She's a hangin' and a haulin' clothes all over this little town—she goes from house to house with her bundle much like Santa in December. Then we got this ex-school teacher from Missouri who cleans these little houses. Course he works for nuthin'. A mighty high educated feller he is, too. Says money ain't import to him cuz he fits a cog in the big machinery of building a wonderful, heavenly place over yonder on the Muddy.

And some of you kindly folk out there in newspaper

land have been readin' some mighty spirited stuff about our good farmer Dave Dickson tellin' these red-garbed folk they could have Antelope for their consarn businesses, whatever they might be, suh, but Dave ain't that kinda' fella whose gonna set the devil onto his kinfolk and friends.

Dave has a lovely little woman, Melinda. They live under the same roof with a couple of little Dicksons. These good parents ain't gonna let nobody tell them that their kiddies should be shunted off into a dormitory with a lot of other little folks, away from their mommy's evercaring eye. No siree, these Dicksons are straight away thoughty parents, thriving in the free enterprise system. They's gonna see that someone of blood tucks them offspring in at night, not some strange person of the "free labor" society. The little Dicksons is taken every Sunday to Sunday school by Dave hisself.

A more honest kinda guy you wouldn't find than ole Dave. If'n he was to tell you today that he had sold 59 head of cattle, then by tomorrow when the brand inspector was to show up to check those critters, by jimminy, there'll still be 59 not 48! If this Dave says a word or two that kinda' jerks up the folks over there on the Muddy, maybe it's because he has fatherly hopes of his little boys adoing some ranchin' for theirselves, right there on that same claim where their granddaddy farmed. Now I do declare that's worth a scrap or two!

Other folks don't seem to think so much of little guys and gals even being borned. I heard say that the head mogul over there is tellin' those little ladies to get rid of their babies even before they draws their first breath!

Yeah, too bad all the mommies and daddies ain't as careful who tuck their little ones in at night, feels their brow for fever, or listens to, "Now I lay me down to sleep" with a bit of glisten in the eye.

And so I do leave you now with just a mite more—you shouldn't believe all that bad stuff about us'n here in Antelope.

We are just trying to exist, and be good, loving neighbors

as we have for years; howsome ever it would be appreciated a
bit if these beloved new folks would mow their lawns, cuz the
hard working, hard riding, honest to goodness word keepin'
gentry before them always did.
   And so for now, from me to you, I remain,
   Signed Merry Sunbeam O'Day
   (Following this letter, the lawns in Antelope were
mowed.)
   Throughout all the stress-filled days sufficient incidents
of humor occurred, some by chance and others contrived,
which stiffened our backbones for the next onslaught. The
Bosswhan of Eagle Canyon (Herb McKay) planned just such a
happy event.
   After suffering through two summers of thousands of
followers trooping through the valley in order to congregate
at the Muddy for the Bhagwan's annual money-making festival, it was appropriate that a non-Rajneesh celebration be
held. Bosswhan McKay's wife Cheeka and her neighbor Rosemary planned the fun-filled day. Invitations were mailed to
all the Descendants of Pioneers. Underneath a picture of the
guru (Bosswhan McKay), the invitation said:

Beloved Donna, Love,

CALLING THE FAITHFUL TO THE FEET OF THE
ENLIGHTENED ONE!!

The Bosswhan of the Church of the Descendants of Or-
egon Pioneers requests your presence in celebration of
Master's Day on Sunday, July 17, 1983, at Clarno, Oregon. The
joining of our voices and actions in vibrant meditation will
generate enormous energy in honor of the Master. Many ac-
tivities have been planned:
   2 pm - Baseball game at Bosswhanfield (McKay alfalfa)
   5 pm - Barbecue at Master's Temple (McKay home)
   7 pm - Music at Church of the Descendants of Oregon
      Pioneers (Clarno Grange)

*On the hour - informal viewing tour of the great 1983
Muddy Ranch/Clarno Burn
Continuously - Videotapes of the prior year's television
services
Beer, hamburgers and trimmings, and table service will
be provided, but a church cannot operate without donations,
for your tithe you are expected to contribute either a dessert
or salad.
His Blessings,
Signed Bosswhan Herb McKay.*

Unable to attend, due to pretrial hearings in Portland, I
sent the following reply in Rajneesh jargon, as I knew it.

*Beloved Bosswhan, Too much dynamic meditation has
rendered your abject subject powerless to respond to your call
to aggregate energy flow on Sunday, July 17.
This mindless person is in an abyss of negativity due to
an over expenditure of positive energy generated recently on
behalf of those in Antelope Valley.
My tithe to you has been needed by bellwire Mother, and
has been there sent, unwillingly and with definite feelings of
negativity.
Like the pioneers up Eagle Canyon, this person would
give acey deucy energy to you on this esoteric day, but quiet
meditation overcomes all.
May your enlightenment be heard and seen throughout
Rhada River Country and encase Rhada folks with great
negativity.
Signed, Donna*

By this date, the Rajneeshees had renamed the John Day
River the Rhada River just as they had changed the name of
Antelope to Rajneesh and given all the streets new names.

TEN

"Remember, Donna, you will be under oath just as if you were in the witness box in the courtroom. Swami Niren will be seeking information to use against you when we go to trial."

It was September 1, 1983. Garry McMurry was preparing me for the first day of deposition, a new experience for me. I was to learn from this new experience that once I had filed the lawsuit against the Rajneesh Foundation, et al, I made myself a pawn in the legal game, and the judges and lawyers would direct all my moves.

Being deposed by the defendant's attorney is tantamount to providing a stranger with the keys to one's personal diary in order for the stranger to gather information with which to manipulate. A deposition is a forceful tool wrested from an unwilling litigant.

Today I felt secure and at ease. Certainly I had nothing to hide, and I was well protected from whatever might befall—protected by two learned gentlemen.

We sat with our backs to the windows in Mr. McMurry's council chambers. He sat to my left, a man of average stature, but greater than average charm. Handsome features, generous nose, silver hair and a demeanor that elicited respect and consideration from all he encountered. He never walked, but rather glided smoothly as if hinged with ball bearings. His office was close enough to the courthouse for us to walk to and fro. He covered the distance like an athlete even though handicapped with two heavy briefcases.

He could have been an equally successful actor. He was completely in charge and in control of his lines: however, in his private office he might be caught off guard, out of control, and almost volatile on those occasions when an elusive document was not readily found on his cluttered desk.

Carrell F. Bradley, white-haired genius with an I.Q. of 178, sat to my right. A man of such intellect and regiment he provided no time for unnecessary chitchat during business hours, but at lunch he was apt to entertain me with an original, humorous Bhagwan poem.

It was always a pleasure to sit across from him in his law office in Hillsboro, Oregon; however, about the time I would be thoroughly enjoying our exchange of thoughts, he would tactfully conclude the meeting. Sometimes I left knowing that what I had had to say was of no consequence to my defense, and so he had no time to listen.

Mr. Bradley's scrubbed, round face carries all the innocence of youth, but underneath his disarming exterior, at the ready, is the courage, will and capability of a dragon slayer. At our first meeting, I judged him as a hard man without emotion, but later I discovered he had a sincere desire to protect and encourage. I liken him to the regal German shepherd dog to whom one does not extend a hand until invited to do so. He provided wonderful ballast on the days of deposing.

So the three of us waited for Swami Niren (Phillip Toelkes) of Rajneesh Legal Services to arrive. At twenty minutes after ten, Mr.. McMurry called the Rajneesh Hotel and was told the irritating news— Niren was on his way to California. Had he forgotten?

Five minutes later the telephone rang. Niren would be there shortly. Twenty-five minutes later, "Garry, what I do in a case like this is go about my business and bill the lawyer for one hour of my service," the busy Mr. Bradley said. At that moment a breathless Niren appeared, alone. Where was the usual tattler that accompanies a Rajneeshee on an important mission?

A youthful, good-looking man, square face, hard-set jaw, a generous mouth with a pouty lower lip and eyes so dark it was impossible to differentiate between pupil and iris, and today as he arrived a long, straight lock of black hair drooped over his right forehead. He removed his plum-colored jacket to expose large sweat stains under his arms. He was indeed nervous, ill-prepared and generally disheveled, an observation which further allayed my fears.

We exchanged greetings, He sat down, removed a cloth pouch from his briefcase and from the pouch took a chunk of clear rock crystal and placed it on the table in front of me. It was about five inches tall, obelisk in shape with a flat prism of one-inch at the base. The sun shining over my shoulder from the windows behind reflected brightly on the prism.

I knew I wasn't going to give any of my attention to his rock, and so I pushed a large box of written material between it and me. Niren quickly moved the box away to expose the rock, and I again put the box back and said, "I don't care to look at your rock or whatever it is." He grinned slightly and took from his trouser pocket what sounded like a stone as he placed it on the table before him. I was remembering that the Bhagwan is considered one of the world's greatest hypnotists. Are his emissaries also schooled in the ways of mesmerism?

The questioning began. Strange questions. The size of the lot where I lived. Was it fenced? Did the neighbors wave to me as they drove by? As I answered his questions, I endeavored never to mention a name, because I did not want to implicate anyone, but it was inevitable that names would be divulged, and so I jotted down the initials of that person in order to remember to tell them of the particular conversation with Niren. He asked for the pad. I had to give it to him, and from it he got more ideas for further questions. Several friends from the Antelope Valley were subpoenaed as a result.

Actually, the first day of deposition was uneventful compared to January 17, 1984 when Niren arrived late again with an entourage of Rajneeshees who crowded into the council chamber.

A heated discussion ensued between the attorneys which required a ruling from Multnomah County Judge Crookham who decided that a paralegal, Swami Shanananda, and the commune president, Ma Prem Vidya, could stay. Niren directed Vidya to sit across the table from me. The others had to leave.

Vidya placed a rock crystal on the table, picked up a gold pen and began a rhythmic tapping as she stared at me—glassy-eyed—without blinking and without expression! I tried to break her stare and could not, nor could I get any change of expression from her bulging eyes which were disconcerting by their very structure. Because she was hard-core Rajneeshee from the administrative office in Poona, India, I felt a hidden threat in her presence.

Niren placed his rock on the table. I had with me that day Bob Larson's book on cults, and so I stood it open in front of Vidya's crystal, and I placed my briefcase on the table in front of Niren's rock. Even though I could no longer see the crystals, Niren constantly reminded me that his was there by looking at it before and after each of his questions. During one recess, Vidya said, "See this beautiful crystal? It is a very strong crystal!"

We had begun about 10:25 a.m. At exactly 11 a.m. Cynthia Chandler, Mr. McMurry's secretary, entered with a note which he read aloud into the stenographer's record. "Several sannyasins are in the lobby with foodstuffs, and they wish to serve them in here." He responded with a definite "no" and left for the foyer.

Mr. Bradley and I followed. Sure enough, halved grapefruit each sporting a maraschino cherry, and muffins, cookies, sweet rolls, and beverage were being served with fine gold flatware and ivory-colored china trimmed in plum color.

Mr. McMurry ordered them and their "picnic" out of the reception area while Niren enjoyed a pastry. No one moved toward the door, and so again Judge Crookham had to be called in order the eject the pantry crew. Both attorneys spoke with him. Niren berated Mr. McMurry for not permitting him a cup of coffee. To the judge he cleverly reduced the sumptuous repast down to a simple cup of coffee. The judge promised to locate an empty jury room, in the neutral territory of the courthouse, for us to use in the afternoon.

Throughout all pretrial hearings and the trial, too, we would see female Rajneeshees with foodstuffs on hand. I deduced the reds had no pocket money with which to feed themselves. A natural assumption since I had read in the

Rajneeshee Times that Niren was very happy to have closed out his last personal back account. (Ma Prem Karuna, the first Rajneeshee mayor of Antelope, was the only overweight sannyasin I ever saw.)

The morning was wasted much to Mr. Bradley's chagrin; after-all, he had already been exposed to the interruptive caterers during Rosemary's hearing.

At 2:00 p.m. we were in Judge Crookham's court again. He said a jury room would not be available until 2:45, but in the meantime he ruled "no crystals on the conference table." Niren protested and persisted, "It's a religious artifact, Your Honor." (Deny them anything, and you deny them their right to religious freedom!) "No different from the cross Ms. Quick is wearing," he continued.

The judge, with a twinkle in his eyes, said, "You are wearing a religious artifact around your neck, (the mala) and I will rule one artifact per person."

So it was late that January day when we got down to the business at hand. Vidya across the table began the steady tapping with her pen and assumed the uncanny stare. She stopped the tapping long enough to write Niren notes after which the three of them would laugh at the contents. Her note paper bore a picture of her master. Very adroitly she maneuvered two of these in front of me.

I knew pictures of the Bhagwan existed everyplace and anyplace where his followers might possibly be. Even on a trip to a toilet at the commune, whether one sat or stood, his large eyes watched the action.

Shanananda stared, too, and when our eyes met, he would widen his to the maximum, hold that position and then close them. How queer!

It was nearly four o'clock before Niren got around to asking questions that were pertinent and not repetitious. Mr. Bradley had to leave, and a strong feeling of lethargy enveloped me. Vidya's stare and metronomic tapping sufficiently unnerved me. "Niren, you should bring with you those whose countenances are pleasant. These people look at me with extreme hatred." He reminded me that I had not endeared them to me with the million-dollar lawsuit. Then Vidya stopped the tapping, took the picture of the Bhagwan that hung from the end of her mala and used it to scribe an arc directly under her right eye. This she did in a steady cadence. I had stopped looking at her, but the movement was always apparent to me. I believed these actions—her tapping, staring and swinging the picture of the Bhagwan and Shanananda's queer eye movements were all choreographed earlier and were intended to disrupt my concentration.

The most devastating and dehumanizing experience was yet to come.

Scarcely a week before trial date, I was informed that a psychiatric and physical examination had been scheduled. Both were to be conducted by the Bhagwan's doctors.

I laughed as I told my attorneys I would have to be marching to a looney-tune in order to take the psychiatric exam seriously. "How can a man who believes in a living god, whose religious philosophy espouses a sexual route to the highest religious attainment possibly access my thinking processes?"

I found this both absurd and humorous. I laughed. That was my last laugh for many days to come.

The Rajneeshees now had the upperhand. The defendant in a lawsuit has the right to engage a doctor of choice to ascertain if, indeed, an injury has been sustained. When that law was written, did the lawmakers anticipate that entering the legal arena would come a destructive cult with membership including licensed physicians?

Certainly a conflict of interest was flagrantly evident, and the Bhagwan's spokespeople had repeatedly exhibited a penchant for strangling the truth whenever the truth was an obstacle to their plans.

Ron Wade, Mr. McMurry's assistant, accompanied me to the Rajneesh hotel, where we found the lobby full of the Bhagwan's hierarchy including City Slick.

Swami Siddha, the psychiatrist kept us waiting. When

he did appear, he advised us that this examination would require eight hours—another nuance to lead to my complete vexation.

I accompanied him through the lobby and up a short flight of stairs into a narrow room about fourteen feet long with one window on the street. Its blind was closed. Light was scant. He directed me to sit in the chair at the end of a small table, and then he turned on a blinding flood light which had already been positioned to shine into my face. Next to it was the lens of a video camera. He sat behind the desk next to the light.

The narrow room appeared to be used as a library. The left wall was shelves, and as my eyes adjusted, I could see some of the writings of the Bhagwan in evidence, but there were no certificates or degrees authorizing the practice of medicine. I told Siddha I was accustomed to seeing these documents. He explained his office was at the ranch. Did I want to postpone this examination until he could get them? Of course I did not.

Since it was a sunny August day, I suggested the blind be opened in order to dispense with the spotlight. "The equipment requires the light just as it is." We sat looking at each other in awkward silence. I was to become particularly aware of long silences and the penetrating gaze of his unblinking eyes as the morning progressed.

Suddenly he began to open and squint his eyes just as the paralegal, Shanananda, had done. What was he trying to accomplish? Finally I felt compelled to break the staredown. "If you have questions for me, why don't you get started so we can get this thing over with?" He did.

In a soft monotone voice he began asking about my birth. How much did I weigh? Was I full term? Was it a difficult birth? Was I breast fed? His early questions I could not answer not did I understand their relevance.

I was determined to maintain eye contact with him even though that meant the camera caught my full face, and I was pleased that I could remain passive. Then he spoke of death and funerals. Remembering the recent memorial for a friend brought tears to my eyes. As I wiped away those tears and blew my nose, I apologized for the interruption. Then I saw how satisfied he was to have discovered my Achilles heel.

After three hours of being questioned in a soft, monotone voice with regular intervals of silence—always in conjunction with strange eye movement—we returned to the lobby at which time Siddha told Ron that I had to be back after lunch.

Once out on the street, I began spouting my anger at being treated like a criminal undergoing an inquisition. I told the attorneys I would not be subjected to a session with Siddha again.

Mr. McMurry said I must or the judge would dismiss the case. "Let the case be dismissed then!" I said. I was adamant.

Again at 2:00 p.m. we were in Judge Crookham's court.

Mr. McMurry described the hostility in the hotel and the environment in the examination room. The judge questioned Siddha, particularly about the lighting. Siddha lied, said only indirect lights were used. Then he asked for a total of eight hours with me. The judge granted his request.

Sometimes it seemed that Judge Crookham favored the Rajneeshees in his rulings; however, I believed they were just and intended not to provide a loophole wherein the Rajneesh lawyer could later file for another trial due to a biased ruling against them.

The next morning as Ron and I walked to the neutral turf of the courthouse, he kindly tried to bolster my morale. "Look at it this way, Donna. You'll get to tell the jurors all that has happened to you." (I never did get that opportunity.) ""It will mean a bigger judgement."

We stepped into the juror's room, and there it was—the indirect lamp which Siddha had described to Judge Crookham the day before. "Oh, you have a different light today," I said.

"Ms. Quick, this is the same light you saw yesterday?"

"Why did you lie to the judge?" I asked.

"Ms. Quick, do people often lie to you?" he asked, reflecting upon my competency.

"No, only Rajneeshees," I snapped.

Again he directed me to a chair at the end of the table, and had it not been for Ron I would have had to sit in that vulnerable position. Until yesterday, I never knew that a mere table could be a bulwark.

Today I chose to be angry. I knew I was not going to be intimidated, and I knew I was not going to cry. I would neither look at him nor allow him to look at me. A large brimmed hat was my buffer. His camera caught only my chin and the top of the hat; furthermore, I wrote notes at random to occupy my hands. He was irritated. Good!

"Ms. Quick, what are you writing?"

"Notes for future reference." Today I was in charge. When he returned to the topic of funerals, as I knew he would, I was without emotion.

About eleven o'clock he gave me the Multiphasic Personality Inventory test which consists of series of questions with multiple choice answers. I purposely began answering with a pen until he instructed me to use a pencil. Then I suspicioned that my pencil marks might be changed in order to provide them with answers that would serve their purpose.

Within two months of the Rajneeshee's arrival in north central Oregon, we in the Antelope Valley knew they should always be held in suspect. Unfortunately, it took nearly two years to convince some politicians that our finds were accurate—our concerns well-founded.

The second day with Siddha was to conclude at 11:30. At precisely that time Ron walked into the room, saw I was busy and quietly took a seat at the end of the room. Siddha ordered him to leave—said he was a disruptive force. Ron asked him how he could be considered an intrusion if he sat in silence. An altercation ensued. When I found a break in their verbal exchange, I told Siddha, "He doesn't bother me."

Ron remained. "Give me back my test, Ms. Quick." Eager to complete it, I ignored him. "I want my test back." I ignored him.

"I shall have to call Rajneesh Legal Services." He would threaten us. His words came in rapid, high-pitch frustration. He hurried toward the door only to stop there and return just as quickly. I doubt he had a quarter for the telephone.

How amusing it was to observe this man so perplexed over such a small matter—a situation he had created. He was not accustomed to having his orders rebuffed.

Siddha was a VIP in the Bhagwan's territory where will-fulness was not tolerated. The followers of the Bhagwan were well indoctrinated in the ways of abject obedience, but Ron and I did not share their desire to please. We both refused to comply with Siddha's orders—a turn of events he could not handle. This was not the first time I had observed a Rajneeshee spokesperson at a loss of direction when a new tack was introduced for which they were not previously pro-grammed.

I completed the test at 11:45 p.m.

"You'll have to come back tomorrow, Ms. Quick."

"Oh, no," I stated. "You have had your day with me, and you'll not see me again." Because of these words, he instigated another hearing before Judge Crookham at 1:00 p.m., where he told the judge that Ron interfered with my completion of the examination, and the last half had to be repeated. The judge ruled in his favor.

The next morning we met again in Mr. McMurry's of-fice. I needlessly answered the questions for a second time. That afternoon I completed the identical test for an accom-modating doctor who located the "outdated and seldom-used" test for me in order to provide insurance against any tamper-ing with my answers in the first one.

Siddha had had his way throughout our association.

That afternoon I suffered extreme chest pains due to anxiety; due to the rigorous schedule of these pretrial hear-ings; and due to what I felt were permissive judicial rulings.

That same day, Dr. Shanyo, one of at least eight physi-cians who were adherents to Rajneeshism, met me at my doctor's office in St. Helens, Oregon. (Dr. Dory Walrod) I had insisted she be present at all times. There was very little "touching." His examination of me was another inquisition, another fact-finding session.

Like Dr. Siddha, he tried to get me to say that the chest pains I had experienced while caring for my mother had continued through the years. Of course that was not the case. When my mother was no longer my patient, the chest pains ceased, and did not return until I was embroiled with the Rajneeshees.

When he asked if I deliberately did those things that might trigger pain, I told him I weighed the importance of the event and acted accordingly. I do not intend to outlived my usefulness.

He dwelt at length on my anxiety. "Anything about anxiety you want to mention?"

"Yes. I said to Donald one day, 'Donald, do you ever look up at the flag at the schoolhouse and think that yes, this really is America just to remind yourself that we aren't in some foreign country?' And he said, 'absolutely.' Now that sir, is anxiety."

The Bhagwan's emissaries—his attorneys and his doctors—served him well, but not without serving me, too. They maneuvered me into strong character-building events.

I knew of their devious tactics, and I believed the visitor to Oregon from India who said Americans are easy prey to the practitioners of hypnotism, and so I was ever cognizant of the Swamies' oblique behavior. I knew it was probable that those few of us who consistently attempted to thwart their plans could be targets for mesmerism.

What I did not know was that the system of justice would give to them every advantage, give to them every edge in order to be assured there would be no outcry of prejudice.

Dr. Shanyo's conference with me was audio-taped and except for dangerously high blood pressure—that was to be expected—I was found in excellent health.

Throughout my life I have never joined those people who have yearly medical checkups. My attitude has always been one of prevention, and unless I break a bone or cut an artery, I will not seek the care of a physician, but when Janet told me she thought I had heart disease, I relented and called the nearby Doctor Walrod of St. Helens only to learn that she was not taking any new patients, and so I went to the doctor she recommended.

He ordered an electrocardiogram at the hospital, and I went home. Soon he called and asked me to return to get a prescription. I did, and he told me I had already had a heart attack according to the EKG, and he said I must keep with me at all times nitro glycerin tablets. "Take one at the onset of the pain. If it continues, take another tablet in ten minutes, and then get yourself to the hospital." He further instructed me to see a heart specialist whom he recommended.

In all of my years I have appreciated unusually good health and immunity, and today, because I visited a doctor, I learn that I am seriously ill! "I'm the healthiest heart patient ever to sit across the desk from you, Doctor Rush. My entire medicine cabinet consists of a box of bandaids and a small bottle of merthiolate," I told the specialist. "You're far beyond that now, young lady," he added to my anxiety. "But my trouble is in my head," I insisted. "Whenever I get embroiled in Rajneeshee activities—even to see them on the television— that's when my chest hurts." He ignored that comment, went to a diagram of a heart on the wall and unfolded to me his views of the operation which he said I needed. He said my heart would not stand a stress test. He prescribed a calcium blocker medication. I never took it.

Several days passed with the chest pain persisting especially at night when my thoughts were of the pending trial. That pain, in addition to the frightening news from two doctors that I was indeed a heart-attack victim, aggravated my anxiety and caused me to believe I was about to die one terrible morning.

My good neighbor took me to the hospital, where I submitted to an arteriogram which substantiated what I had said—my heart is a healthy heart. Four thousand dollars later

I was dismissed, "Go home and have your esophagus checked," the specialist said.

The pains persisted. I pleaded with Dr. Walrod to take me as a patient, and she did. The EKG's she took did not indicate a previous heart attack or a heart abnormality! Her announcement that I was a healthy women, removed my anxiety and affected immediate relief.

ELEVEN

The jurors were selected August 13, the first day of trial.
Mr. McMurry, Ron and I were content. We had a good panel.
I sat between them and had great faith all would go well, and
we would prevail. I had reviewed all the material we would
enter as evidence and felt prepared to expose facts to the jurors
who would then see the Rajneeshees as aggressive, untruthful
and willing to apply any method to destroy their critics, so
how could any Rajneeshee testimony be credible?

Ma Anand Sheela was Mr. McMurry's first witness. She
refused to swear an oath upon the Bible to uphold the truth,
and all subsequent Rajneeshee witnesses took that oath upon
the book of Rajneeshism. (All the books of Rajneeshism were
later ceremoniously burned upon the Bhagwan's orders at
which time he declared there was no such religion!)

Sheela was cute and evasive, continually told the judge
she couldn't answer with a simple yes or no, and she didn't. At
one point she turned to the judge and said, "McMurry winked
at me, do I have to answer that question?" I remember when
Ron deposed her how haughty her attitude and caustic her
remarks. He displayed extreme patience—even when she
questioned his ability.

I liked Ron, a young man of six foot six with the
rounded shoulders often seen in unusually tall men. He was
all legs and brains, and I so labeled him.

The day he deposed Sheela at the Rajneesh Hotel in Portland, he and Mr. McMurry stepped into the hall to confer. I
followed them as far as the door when I realized I should stay
in the room where they had left their briefcases. City Slick
came in and closed the door behind him whereupon they all
focused on me and broke into song, chanting an ode to the
Bhagwan.

Ron was missing from the courtroom on the fourth day.
I missed him and his helpful suggestions one of which should
have been implemented. He said that Rosemary should tes-

tify that Judge Olsen had found Sheela's letter defamatory and had awarded her damages. Rosemary had already offered to testify. His suggestion went unheeded, even though my lawsuit was based on that same letter.

Mr. McMurry and I sat alone. Niren was surrounded by Rajneeshees. Even those behind the bar sent him frequent notes. There was much activity in the audience. An assortment of onlookers came daily. One lady brought snacks and a thermos. Rajneeshees were plentiful. Those who came differed from day to day and must have been assigned seats, again, leaving no more than three seats for unreds with a Rajneeshee listener occupying the middle seat in the row behind.

My special friends were a welcome sight sitting in the sea of red. Janet, Pat Cox and Jean Opray, all of Antelope, were there every day. I knew it was difficult for them—listening to the lies, when they knew the truths. Raye Reynolds came one day and gave me a kiss on the cheek which said a thousand words.

People unknown to me offered support. Sometimes I would find notes on the table when I took my seat. A young attorney, Charles Thomas Boardman, gave me his card one day with words of encouragement. Pat Lear of Lear Enterprises came for two days, and following that meeting we became pen pals. She had had her own legal bout with the cultists.

The atmosphere in the courtroom was electric. Sheela had been photographed with a pistol on her belt, and some of us wondered if she wore it beneath her overblouse. One day the judge jerked to attention when a friend of mine from Corvallis half stood up in order to remove her coat. Toward the end of the trial, two armed guards were assigned to stand against the wall at the end of the jury box, and on the last day, everyone was ordered to remain seated until the jurors had time to leave the building.

The Rajneeshees deliberately intimidated Janet and Jean—no doubt because they were residents of Antelope and didn't hide their disdain for the reds. A male sannyasin was assigned to sit next to Janet, and whenever possible they maneuvered themselves into the four seats that surrounded her. She spoke with Judge Olsen about the activities in his courtroom, and when she came out of his chambers, Jean Opray went in with similar complaints.

Swami Niren was then asked to step into the judge's chambers. That was the only time he was not accompanied by Mr. McMurry when the judge called a conference. Niren then spoke with several of the sannyasins in the audience, and the days that followed were not so stressful for my friends.

I knew that Jean was a keen observer to the trial proceedings, since she and her husband had engaged an attorney to file a lawsuit for them against the Rajneeshees for unlawful arrest.

Jim and Jean were the only remaining residents of Antelope who openly persisted in opposing the Rajneeshee presence in town. She attended and recorded each of their council meetings. Often she was the only non-Rajneesh in attendance.

Jim picketed the Rajneesh police force by carrying a large placard up and down Main street. He attracted much attention and evoked anti-Rajneesh publicity. The Rajneeshees took steps to stop them.

At 10:00 p.m. one night, five members of the police force forcibly entered their home, handcuffed him and took him to the county seat, The Dalles, eighty-seven miles away. By the time they arrived a goodly crowd of sympathizers met them on the courthouse steps.

The police had no warrant nor any other authority to substantiate their action. The Oprays had turned on the tape recorder with the first knock on their door, and they had recorded all the hysterical verbal exchange as Jean asked them by what right were they arresting her husband. They had a contrived charge, but no warrant, although they said they had orders from the district attorney to bring him in. None of this was true.

The Oprays felt they had a pat case against the Rajneeshee police force, and my defense attorney, Carrol Bradley, told me he would like to handle the lawsuit for them, but they had already hired an attorney in The Dalles. For a reason unknown to anyone but that attorney, the statute of limitations passed without a lawsuit filed!

Those of my friends who were there in the courtroom everyday noticed, as I did, that the judge kept his mind uncluttered by gazing at the ceiling, and so he missed some of the repulsive performances by Sheela. She gave Laura Bentley an obscene finger gesture more than once. Laura was the coordinator of Concerned Oregonians in Wasco County and was responsible for several rallies dedicated to informing county residents of the dangers of Bhagwan's political power. (They would learn firsthand later.)

She took the witness stand for me as did ex-mayor Margaret Hill, Floyd McKay, news anchorman for television station K.G.W. testified in my behalf along with John Silvertooth-Stewart (Janet's son), journalist Bill Driver and Donald Smith.

Mr. McMurry had scheduled a lifelong friend of my mother to be a character witness in my behalf and an ex-Rajneeshee to testify as to the inner-workings of the cult, but he never called them to the witness box. I was beginning to feel that he was too complacent. I wanted to give them all the big guns we had.

Dr. Walrod told him she admired what I was doing, but she did not want anything to do with "those people." She had already told me to be ready to lose because "money talks." I asked Mr. McMurry to subpoena her, but he said he never subpoenaed a doctor who was not a willing witness.

My doctor from Madras, Dr. Bud Beamer, was a splendid witness for me, but he was denied the use of Dr. Walrod's records: however, the Rajneeshee doctor had access to them. Why? A point of law, perhaps, which I did not understand.

During the first week of litigation, Sees Chocolate Company made extra sales of one pound boxes of candy which were sent to all the outstanding opponents of the Bhagwan, even Mr. McMurry's secretary received one. He and I got a bouquet of flowers. "They're going to explode any minute now." He laughed.

Another interesting coincidence took place the first week of July that year when a young couple spooning in Portland's Washington Park rose garden encountered another couple gathering many long-stemmed roses. When the young man asked them what they thought they were doing, they stared as Rajneeshees on assignment and continued picking the choice blooms. Two days later we viewed the Bhagwan's Rolls Royce being festooned with longstemmed roses as his followers paid him homage at the height of a celebration.

Earlier the same year the Oregonian carried an article that outlined a special request the Rajneeshees made to the state's Department of Commerce wherein they asked for forty-eight hours notice before an official from that bureau was to make an official premise visit to Rajneeshpuram. The department head refused. On another page of the same paper was a news item about a noxious gas of unknown origin that permeated the office of the Department of Commerce which caused an abrupt exodus of ailing employees!

Whenever a Rajneesh request was denied, retribution followed. The United Parcel Service driver who delivered to Rajneeshpuram was told to pull off the road and wait until the Bhagwan's car and his entourage passed before venturing on. He refused. Two letters of complaint were immediately sent to the UPS office in Portland, but he was supported by his superiors. His fellow drivers gave him the honorary title of "Driver of the Year."

I experienced a terrorizing act of intimidation in the courthouse. Friends and I had eaten lunch upstairs, where I inadvertently left my suit jacket. Once back on the fifth floor, I missed it and dogtrotted down the hall to wait for an elevator. When one arrived Rajneeshees filed out. I got into the empty lift, and a Swami followed. As soon as the door closed, he took from his pocket a switchblade knife. I heard and saw the steel as it left its case. The eighth floor came not any too soon. I got out, and he remained for the trip down. I should have visited the judge's chambers, too, with an accounting of that incident. I did tell Mr. McMurry who made no comment.

That afternoon while in the witness box, I found an opportunity to say, "The Bhagwan says you have to be ready to kill, to murder if you want to succeed in this world." Niren came half out of his seat to object and decided otherwise. I remembered telling their psychiatrist that I had read the Bhagwan's book The Sound of Running Water, and so Niren knew I could recite the entire quote which clearly states the Bhagwan's amoral attitude toward violence.

The judge soon declared me a "public person" thereby making it extremely difficult to prove they had defamed me. He based his decision on the many public appearances I had made against the Rajneeshees and the numerous letters published in the newspapers. Niren supplied him with all the details of my activities.

Judge Olsen rejected much of the evidence which I had used as reference material for speeches, i.e. a Life magazine which featured the cult in an investigative report; a copy of the eastern paper, SoHo News, containing information about the cult while they were headquartered in New Jersey; letters from parents who had lost children to Bhagwan. And to the contrary, Niren was privileged to present the ugly video of the Madras confrontation and excerpts out of context that favored his case.

I hung my head in great humiliation as he played that video of the confrontation that took place at the Bhagwan's turnaround at the edge of Madras. The jurors viewed it in its entirety.

The judge did not disallow it nor did my attorney object to it on the grounds of relevancy. Without interruption the lengthy, scandalous film rolled to the end. The film had nothing to do with me or any other resident of Antelope. The Rajneesh's propaganda experts scored again. They planned, choreographed and presented the evidence without hindrance!

At its conclusion, my attorney stood up and told the judge he would move for a mistrial, if we were not so near the end. In my heart, I believed we should have taken whatever action necessary to stop their presentation of slanderous, unrelated evidence. I wondered if his decision to do nothing was based on his belief that we would win in any event, or did he not want to cost his law firm the added expense for a new trial? He had told me at the onset that it would cost me nothing, and except for two statements for depositions taken, I never received a bill from him. (Vidya's deposition $266.25 and Sheela's $573.55.) I do remember on one of my first visits to his office, he showed me a lawbook that stated that an attorney could not pay all the expenses for a client.

Mike Sullivan, District Attorney for Jefferson County was the next witness called in my behalf. Mr. McMurry questioned him about the mayhem at the turnaround point in Madras and whether or not I was there. His answer was not decisive. He was a weak witness. Much later I learned that an attempt had been made on his life sometime before my trial date. Perhaps that affected the tenor of his testimony.

I would have preferred Sheriff Perkins as a witness to relate the details of the mad Madras gatherings, but I was not made privy as to those who were to testify in my behalf. Ham stood up to Sheela when she told him, "If you want to see a show of force, I can give you a show of force." And he was successful in convincing her it was prudent for her boss to take a different route, and so he did—right through Antelope on its Main street and on beyond to the ghost town of Shaniko.

Swami Niren played another video as evidence against me—that of my first speech in Redmond in April of 1982, but this time he stopped it midway through and stated that that was all they had.

I told Mr. McMurry the jurors must have the opportunity to see it all, because in the latter half I defended their right to practice any religion in any way. I also expressed sympathy for his followers and told the Rotarians that I entertained the idea of putting a sign on the front gate, "Ex-Rajneeshees Welcome Here" hoping to help some to escape. In that speech I made it clear that Antelope's prime concern was the Rajneesh's political clout due to the ever-increasing number of sannyasins. The Redmond speech would have benefited me, if the jurors had heard it all.

In that speech, I read a letter from a mother whose daughter had become a follower. She wrote, "The Bhagwan is happy when a mother's heart bleeds." Niren attributed the statement to me. Then he aggressively attacked me for stating that perhaps it was their rebirthing chamber in the Rajneesh building on S.E. Hawthorne in Portland where that mother's daughter met the ways of the cult leader.

A rebirthing chamber simulates the womb—a tub filled with tepid water in a sound and lightproof room. Its environment has varied effects, and some participants emerge emotionally sick.

The next morning in the Oregonian one complete page, except for three inches across the bottom, told the history of rebirthing chambers! Niren knew he was going to challenge me on this issue, and the news-type had to have been set and ready to roll in order to accomplish this not-coincidental printing! Yes, Rajneeshees had friends in influential places.

This time the judge refused Niren an opportunity to even attempt to submit his intended evidence. Niren arrived with the paper in hand, and he was about to refer to it when the judge said, "Get that thing out of here."

One day into the second week of trial, I was visiting with friends in the audience during a short recess, when my eyes met with those of a most handsome Swami. A man of perhaps forty years with an engaging smile. "You are new here. Where did you come from?" I flippantly asked. "Come with me, and I'll tell you," he responded, as he pointed to the hallway door. He continued to smile. I continued to look as he bobbed his head forward and backward as far as possible—

again in that steady cadence. I was drawn to look at him.

After court resumed, I was compelled to look over my left shoulder to see him, and each time he bobbed his head as before. I was relieved after two days when a less thought-provoking sannyasin took his seat.

The Rajneeshee seating arrangement in the room was of real interest to my friends. One morning Pat Cox, a regular in attendance, found a pad and pencil placed on a seat next to a friend from Antelope, and so she took it and placed it on another seat and sat down. Soon a swami confronted her. He said that she was sitting in his (assigned) seat. She told him there were other places for him to sit, but he became so loud and belligerent she gave up her position. Later she pointed him out to me. It was Siddha, out of control again because she dared to oppose him.

The lawyers met in the judge's chambers each morning, and the Bhagwan was the critical topic. He had been subpoenaed to appear, and each day he failed to do so. Niren assured the judge that Bhagwan would respond to the court order, but after days of waiting it was obvious he would not.

Another dissident was JoAnne Boies of Albany who was subpoenaed by Niren. She notified the judge by telephone that she would not answer her subpoena until Rajneesh answered his! She was both courageous and correct in her ultimatum. Why shouldn't the law apply equally to all? A question we often asked.

One morning the judge declared he was going to send officers to bring him in, or the plaintiffs should go to the ranch and take his statements. Judge Olsen favored the latter, stating there was a security risk if he came to Portland. Niren must have again used "threats of violence" as the core of his argument for his master to remain at Rajneeshpuram. I wanted to ask the judge, "How about *our* security over there?"

Mr. McMurry had told me he hoped to have the court find the Bhagwan in contempt. He said he would send the transcript to the immigration office, and they could use it as an aid in deporting him. Each day he did not appear, I was more convinced he was on his way back to India, so when my attorney opted to go *to* the ranch, I questioned him. "Now we won't be able to help the immigration office." "But, Donna, I don't want to oppose the judge's suggestion. It will not look good to the jurors." Perhaps he was right.

We were to leave from the Aurora airport early one morning. I bought and used odor-free shampoo and bath soap in order to pass the sniff test everyone was subjected to upon entering the Bhagwan's presence. I would not give them any excuse to separate us once we arrived in the city of reds.

Mr. McMurry and I agreed to meet at the truck stop on I-5 at the Aurora turnoff, but one of us misunderstood, because he never came for me. I wanted to go despite my fears of them en masse.

The video of the Bhagwan's testimony was played for the jurors. He was totally arrogant, rude and abrasive. He aggressively antagonized Mr. McMurry. Upon seeing that video, my immediate wish was that all the world be given the opportunity to see this contemptuous guru make light of the court's order and belittle a member of the Oregon State Bar with audacity, while the honorable judge, via telephone hookup, sat in authority

* * *

An aside here: Many months later there would be a lengthy battle over the ownership of this video of the Bhagwan's deposition. Many people wanted it. The Bhagwan wanted it. Fisher Broadcasting Incorporated and KOIN wanted it. Mr. McMurry wanted it; however, Judge Olsen had ruled that all the plaintiff's evidence belonged to the plaintiff. It was mine!

It was late in January of 1987 that I heard of the hearing scheduled for February 25th before the Oregon Supreme Court. I was filled with dismay that I was never informed of these proceedings—all taking place in my name. I exercised my prerogative and took charge. I dismissed Mr. McMurry and in so doing collected all the files of Quick vs. Rajneesh. In those filed I found letters from Robert J. McCrea, attorney for

Rajneesh Foundation International, in which they offered to
pay me if I would relinquish my right to the film. On one
occasion, he included a copy of the offer and asked Mr.
McMurry to forward it on to me. He did not.

Later in our letters to the Oregon State Bar, Mr.
McMurry said the sum was so little, and he had so much out-
of-pocket expense as a result of the trial, that he felt any
amount collected should be his.

I began communicating with Attorney McCrea about
the tape and finally sold my right to it to Rajneesh Foundation International, but only after I had contacted Jon Tuttle,
newsman of KGW television. I asked for his advice knowing
he was an honorable and respected person. He told me that
should I get it and elect to keep the tape, I should never use it,
and if I sold it, I should not make a copy to keep. I already
knew it was made for the court only, not for anyone's entertainment or exploitation.

* * *

Closing arguments were lengthy. Niren stood for nearly
two hours in front of a four-by-eight sheet of plywood on
which was printed some of the quotes from my letters to the
press, dates of my chest pains and other defendant's material.
I pointed out inaccuracies on the board to Mr. McMurry and
expected him to refute them during his rebuttal. He did not.

Niren delivered punch lines with impact. He was a
learned and skillful adversary. Ron Wade had commented
that it was a great waste of talent for him to limit his career to
the legal needs of his master.

As Niren gave his closing arguments, equating what was
happening to the Rajneeshees as to what Hitler did to the Jews
and emphasizing other incidents completely unrelated to me,
he did something with his body. He stepped back four paces
then forward those same paces, stood in the forward position
a measured length of time then back four paces, etc. (I noted
this to Mr. McMurry.) People often move about while speaking, but his deliberate path and steady timing coupled with
the crystals, pen tapping, squinting and head-bobbing just

added up to more queer, but intentional, behavior.

The quick jury verdict indicated the bad news—a verdict for the defendants. Some of the jurors were crying! What evidence went with them to the deliberation?

At every recess no less than three Rajneeshees sifted through the evidence on the clerk's desk. The bailiff was absent and sometimes the clerk was too. One item submitted which was accepted into evidence was the Sales Catalog of the Bhagwan's writings. I had referred to it several times mentioning titles of his discourses and explanations of others. It was on Niren's desk an entire day. I spoke to the clerk about it and told her I was worried the pages of the old catalog might be substituted with the pages of the new one which had less sexually explicit titles. I wanted the jurors to read, "Leaking Condom" and "Wild Tantra Orgies" and "A Saintly Man Does Not Say F__ or S__."

The verdict emptied the courtroom. Fred Leeson, member of the Oregon State Bar and the newsman who covered the trial for the Oregonian, remained long enough to express his regret and exclaim, "I wanted you to cream 'em."

Janet, Mr. McMurry and I sat alone. "Donna, we have to go and face the press. They will expect you to be in tears." "But what will I say?" I asked. "You can say that you do not think it was fair that the court rejected so many pieces of your evidence," he answered.

Without tears, I told the press that I do believe in the jury system (I hold no malice toward the jurors), and I also mentioned the exclusion of the evidence as Mr. McMurry suggested.

Then the three of us walked back to the law offices. "I should have rebutted, but I thought the jurors had had enough," was Mr. McMurry's lament.

Judge Olsen told the assigning judge he would not hear anymore Rajneesh cases. Could it be because of too much criticism? On her own, my friend Janet mailed him the following letter:

Dear Judge Olsen,

I cannot help but to reflect on the court procedure and findings in the case of Donna Quick vs. Rajneesh and company.

I believe that you as other people in authority are taking our system for granted and you do not recognize the intent of the Rajneeshees. It is not their intent to operate within the framework of our democratic system. They only mange it because we give them concessions. It is their intent to destroy our system and they are using each involvement with our legal and court system to do this. We must become aware of this fact.

I believe you were very permissive in your court procedure with the Rajneeshees and very unfair with Mr. McMurry. You stopped him unnecessarily.

I believe now that it is over and I witnessed your judgement, I am wondering if you are biased, been paid off, scared or too naive to handle the situation. I believe the latter. I could just hear you saying, "I'll just get rid of this article thing before we get the rest of those mentioned in the courtroom." It was the system that was on trial here in the guise of a defamation suit. In the process they both failed. The system certainly failed because you were not in control of it.

I believe that we as Americans are as reported by a reliable source from India, unaware of, do not believe in, or accept mind control, mesmerism or hypnotism, and so we fall easy prey to it. I witnessed mesmerism in your courtroom, when Niren delivered his tirade in the form of a summary. He stepped forward and back in the same pattern as he made his points which took over one and one-half hours. I could not believe my eyes as the jurors sat on the edge of their seats moving back and forth with him. The confrontation episode made in Madras by the Rajneeshees and edited to meet their need and the atrocities perpetrated on the Jews in Germany are about as relevant to Donna Quick as the assassination of J. F. Kennedy. You allowed Niren to subjugate the jurors to guilt by association. If ever their was a mistrial, it seems to me it was here under your supervision.

Where was your bailiff? I saw her only occasionally and only perhaps two times? I was terrified for ten days by these Rajneeshees because of an incident in the courtroom. Niren had the nerve to infer that they needed protection in their freedom of speech while I lost mine right there in your courtroom. The activity within your courtroom was inconceivable. At least two Rajneesh sitting inside the bar during court procedure. As many as five or more hovering over the exhibit's table shuffling through evidence and in the process losing a piece and the Rajneesh bringing in a zerox copy to replace it! Sheela running around the courtroom at recesses sitting on the laps of the male Rajneeshees planted around the room. She was smooching them, kissing and biting lips and ears. She stuck out her tongue, thumbed her nose, and used an obscene gesture more than once.

I was particularly aware of the way you watched the ceiling and seemed completely unaware of the chaos within the room.

I believe the leniency and permissiveness of the court created a miscarriage of justice and defamed two wonderfully intelligent, concerned and extremely fine citizens. The system certainly failed. It failed because no one was guarding it. This is the intent of the Rajneesh to make the system fail.

I just heard on the television that the Rajneeshees are bringing 2,000 people from New York. All this just before elections. Enough to swing the county vote. They are, I believe, sponsoring a woman, Mary Crawford, to run for Wasco County commissioner. I know of no way to stop them.

And regarding the Bhagwan, I believe that you should have done what you would have done to anyone else in his position. You should have arrested him and put him in jail and then he could have been deported. You may never get another chance. Thank you.

Signed, Janet Silvertooth-Stewart.

At the beginning of this letter, I said she wrote this on her own. That is true. Mr. McMurry, in one of his letters to the Oregon State Bar, in answering my complaint stated that I urged Janet and helped write the above. Janet was devastated—just as much as I. The letter was hers alone. After all, she was born in Antelope, accompanied me on every speaking engagement, as well as supporting me on the trip to Washington D.C. This court case was not only mine. It belonged to every freethinking citizen of the state.

It required considerable determination to maintain self-esteem and not crumple under the severe loss of that lawsuit. To give in to the defeat, to cease opposing them on all fronts would be an admission of weakness of character.

A character-building experience it was. When Mr. Bradley, my defense attorney, said the Rajneesh wanted to settle their case against me out of court, I was tempted to protect myself from another depleting courtroom experience, but I couldn't give in to the Rajneeshees. I opted for another trial.

By now those statements I had made which precipitated their case against me were found to be true statements, and again in November of 1984 Bhagwan's lawyer pressed for an out-of-court settlement. I refused. They dropped all charges against me in January of 1985. The Oregonian, on this positive feat for me, printed that a *judge* had dismissed the case! From the first news article to the last, the Oregonian was incorrect; however, Oregonian news reporter Fred Leeson was exemplary in his daily coverage of the trial, and I told him so.

Carrell F. Bradley is a superb lawyer. He protected me from the onset from the Bhagwan's attorneys.

I was grateful for the protective posture he exhibited. Two of his letters to the Bhagwan's attorney sum up his attitude. A paragraph from each follows.

1.) *"August 1, 1984. It appears to me to be decidedly unfair for discovery to be one sided. I cannot understand why the law would require Donna Quick to give her deposition while at the same time you are refusing to produce what I consider to be an important witness on her behalf. Consequently, you may consider this letter as notice that I will not voluntarily produce Donna Quick and should you file a no-*

tice to take her deposition, then I will at the same time notice the Bhagwan's deposition and have him served personally with a subpoena to appear.

2.) "September 4. You ask me tell you what information I want from the Bhagwan so that you can determine whether or not alternate sources are available to obtain that information. I ask the same thing of you for Donna Quick. Tell me what information you want that you do not already have, either through her previous deposition or reading the press clippings or information obtained in her trial, that you want from her, and I will see if alternate sources can be found to get you that information."

Mr. McMurry is an equally good attorney, but with a different approach to matters at hand. A member of the bar who followed the case every day told me, in his opinion, it was quite apparent that McMurry had lost interest in the trial after three days into it. I noticed a decidedly different attitude at the end of the first week. When I took the witness box, he instructed me to take with me my briefcase; however, I never felt that I had time to search for answers in it when Niren was badgering me with his barrage of questions. Several times I floundered trying to answer a charge from Niren. I looked to Mr. McMurry for help. None came. I had hoped on other occasions that he would object to a question. He did not.

The day I told Mr. McMurry about the Rajneeshee who pulled the knife in the elevator, I was dismayed at his lack of concern. I needed a reason, an excuse, a clue for his sometimes indifference, and over two years later I think I found one.

The year we went to court, he was accused of malpractice by the Fred Devine Diving and Salvage, Inc. It involved a failed Saudi Arabian crude oil transaction. It is possible that some of his crucial hearings took place during Quick v. Rajneesh litigation.

Maybe it was I who failed him. He had the utmost faith in me and had told me so. Even with that faith, he dissuaded me from an appeal. The day we lost the case, I asked him about a higher court, but he painted a gloomy picture—telling me my many hours in the witness box would be tripled. And then the day before the statute of limitations would preclude an appeal, he called me. I said, "Let's do it." But he said he had read the entire transcript of the trial and, in his opinion, we did not have a chance.

It was finished.

TWELVE

During the weeks that preceded the trial no controversial news radiated from Rajneeshpuram. The end of the trial was the GO signal, when all Hell broke loose.

The Rajneesh public relations office announced their new entity: THE RAJNEESH HUMANITY TRUST. The Village Voice publication of New York City carried one of its promotional ads which stated: (my words in parenthesis)

"You will need an interest in and desire to participate in this community." (free labor) *"You will need medical insurance and enough money to cover all medical and dental expenses."* (money to be spent with Rajneesh doctors) *"You will need personal spending money."* (to be exchanged for Rajneeshpuram credit)

To further exemplify their philanthropic posture, street people, homeless people, from around the United States were to be transported free of charge by Rajneesh Humanity Trust to the ranch, and most importantly should anyone of these not wish to adopt the communal style of living, that one would be returned home. Rajneesh Humanity Trust did transport many homeless men and women to the ranch; however, after a day and sometimes less, many of them wanted the return ticket, and others who voiced dissent to commune regimen were ordered to a departing bus, but not a bus homeward bound, rather a bus to Madras, The Dalles or Portland.

A nucleus of the first ones dumped on Portland's streets found the Rajneesh Hotel and began picketing on October 8, 1984. Their group leader was Willy Garrison of Boone, North Carolina. The shanghaied pickets hoped to bring attention to their plight and force Bhagwan's people to keep their promise of the ticket home. They could not coerce the Rajneeshees, but they were successful in attracting nationwide attention.

"Janet, we've got to take lunch to those fellows." She agreed. On October 9 we drove to the hotel with the trunk of the car full of sandwiches, boiled eggs, cookies, milk, coffee and oranges. "Another experience." Janet said. Certainly since the arrival of the Bhagwan we had many unplanned experiences and each with its own reward.

That first day, we looked askance at those bewhiskered men. After all, we knew nothing about street people except they were to be found drunk in doorways and under bridges. Each was eager to talk of the bewildering, frightening things they encountered. We listened, and began asking questions. We particularly asked each one if they had registered to vote. All but one said yes. A public-address system at the ranch, placed in the vicinity of the community cafeteria, continually advised, "If you are an American citizen and eighteen years of age, you should register to vote, even if you have not voted

AP/Wide World Photo

Donna Quick talks with John Earle and Richard Laaberd of Cleveland, Ohio who are on the picket line at Hotel Rajneesh, Portland.

before." Bob Burrier of New York City, who was picked up at the Port Authority, Manhattan, had heard Sheela say all who registered would be voters even if they were not there at election time.

Destructive cultists know no bounds to their ability to dominate. Now that the Rajneeshees governed the small town of Antelope, they intended to take over the government of Wasco County! Again, through a preponderance of voters, they would insure their candidate's success in the upcoming election.

David Priddy, of Tulsa, Oklahoma told us he had been chased by a helicopter and snipers on the hilltops had shot at his friend. Berry Rush, Oakland, California told us there was a flu epidemic "over there." It was true, many of them were ill. The Salvation Army brought medicine almost daily, and Janet, accompanied by Robbie Hadder of Denver, walked to the nearby grocery store, where she bought aspirin for the headaches. We felt particular sympathy for young, sad faced Robbie. He told Janet he lived with his mother whom he really missed. He was sorry he had accepted the free bus ride to what he thought was going to be gainful employment. He had been unable to find employment at home. His bus ride terminated on skid road, where he was labeled a streetperson. The Salvation Army came to his rescue four days later, when they put him on a bus for Denver.

We met a married couple Ann and Steve Moranville of Boston, Massachusetts. We had seen her on the news telling how she had been assaulted three times while Steve was restrained. She told me her friend, Amy, had been raped twice. We noticed how solicitous and tender Steve was to her, providing his own worn jacket as a cushion so she might sit more comfortably. We found out she liked chocolate candy, and that's what she got. Later she confided that she was pregnant, and so we were thankful when the Salvation Army found lodging for them until they could send them home to Boston.

Steve told us the Rajneeshees had refused to return his wallet. He was without identification so when an unmarked car picked them up from the hotel sidewalk, we were concerned, especially since Ann was obviously reluctant to go, but upon their return we learned it was a federal agency wishing to question them and have Steve identify weapons he had seen at the ranch. Janet and I had called the Federal Bureau of Alcohol, Tobacco and Firearms to request someone from the office interview the street people, since they had seen automatic weapons, hand grenades and a heat-sensing device on a Rajneesh helicopter.

Michael Sprouse of Jacksonville, California said, "Those people are dedicated and dangerous. They are organized but poorly trained, dedicated and fanatic." He saw a variety of small arms weaponry, including AK 47s, M-Gram 11s with sound and flash suppressors, and Swedish Ks with 18 rounds of .45 caliber ammunition. "These people are serious as heart attacks."

These homeless folks ranged in age from seventeen to past sixty. Jane Louise Barnett of Fort Worth, Texas was collecting her social security. She told me she turned in her two hundred forty dollar check at the ranch and got forty dollars worth of credit in return! We knew that Rajneeshpuram had its own monetary system, and all newcomers were encouraged to turn in U.S. dollars for Rajneeshpuram script.

Jane Louise was sent home to Texas, and I was worried that Rajneeshees had arranged for her future checks to be mailed to the ranch, and so I sent the details to the welfare department in Washington D.C. addressed to Dick Kusserow who had told me he would be interested in receiving information of government checks gone astray; after all, that was one of the reasons for Congressman Ryan's visit to Jonestown.

R. (Riley) C. Whitley from Houston was a new member of the streetpeople society only because of his decision to see the West. "I never saw the west coast and thought I'd just take the roundtrip. Besides, my wife and I had a big fight, and I decided I'd stay out all night, then I saw this bus . . . " After we became better acquainted, he told us that all the new arrivals at the ranch were required to wear an orange bead—the indicator that they had not yet been examined by a Rajneesh doctor. After the physical examination, if they were found to be disease-free, the orange bead was replaced with a blue one, and they were next encouraged to "Go with one of our moms. We've got the best."

Each day when we left them, we assured them we would be back. One day one said to us, "It isn't so much the food. Just support us. We want to go home."

They continued to picket the Rajneesh Hotel for nine days. By then their needs were all being met by the Salvation Army who brought warm jackets, hats and most importantly the bus ticket home. As they left we hugged a couple of our favorites and wished them well. I was happy to receive several kisses on a cheek from fellows labeled streetpeople. We wished them well and I gave my address to two of them hoping to hear good news from them later.

Jerry Robertson and Riley C. Whitley called from Phoenix on their way to Houston. They were ebullient. Their bus had stopped next to a Rajneesh bus where a Humanity Trust recruiter was espousing the benefits of the communal living. Jerry and Riley stepped up and told those listening the story of their trip to the commune where "inhumane, unreal and a sick atmosphere" existed. They were happy because they knew they had discouraged others that day from following in their own misguided footsteps.

The Salvation Army officials, with their dedication of purpose, magnanimously saw to it that over four hundred folks were homeward bound. They did it all without destroying the dignity of the indigents. They were the heroes of the streetpeople-story; but in Albany, Oregon, at the same time the Bhagwan was amassing voters at the commune, JoAnne Boies was gathering voters in her area, voters ready to move to Wasco County and offset the influx of hundreds of streetpeople voters. She and her group marched on the state capital, requested an audience with the governor, were denied, but they stated their intentions to the election officials and to members of the press with such conviction that the

Secretary of State, in order to preserve the integrity of the ballot box, installed election officers at The Dalles who interrogated each and every new registrant.

Just as JoAnne would not answer her subpoena until the Bhagwan answered his, she decided if he could move bonafide voters into Wasco County from around the country so could she move bonafide voters from around the state into the county. The unsung heroine who saved Wasco County from turning all red was JoAnne Boies assisted by Talbot Robinson.

Citizens of Wasco County were anxious and frightened that the Bhagwan's people might have the elective power to move the county seat to Rajneeshpuram. The voter turnout was the greatest Wasco County had ever seen with many new local registrants. Fear, patriotism, and the Bhagwan caused usually apathetic citizens to exercise their right to vote.

Thirteen

There is a special reverence about a small, white country church standing as a sentinel in remote, open rangeland with its bell tower stretching heavenward and all its meaningful structure picturesquely framed by far-off hills.

The simple architecture of the Antelope Community church bespeaks her basic tenet—to offer solace and the unencumbered word of God. Every Sunday morning the timeless hymns from eras past were sung with fervor. Frances Dickson, wife of the postmaster, was the enthusiastic director who could bring forth dulcet offerings from anyone.

The church was built in 1886-87 by the local folks, and proud craftsmen hand-crafted the pews. The deed was held by the Methodist-Episcopal Conference. In its early days, a Reverend traveled from The Dalles to hold monthly services. Sometimes Laura Silvertooth and her friend, Hilme Rooper—with their children—were the only worshippers.

Due to lack of use, the building fell into disrepair, and in 1954 the Methodists planned to dismantle it and sell the pews. But the community, although not in regular attendance, revered their church, and the news that it was soon to be razed united twenty-five local folks. Seven hundred and fifty dollars was donated. The church was purchased and reroofed. The deed was given to the school district to hold in trust.

About 1967 the school district, concerned about liability, turned the deed over to the city to hold in trust, and again, it was in dire need of repairs. Catholics, Methodists and others gave of their time and money to completely overhaul the structure. Reverend Taylor of The Dalles headed the celebration of its restoration on August 7, 1971—its 75th anniversary.

In May of 1982, with the imminent takeover of city government by the followers of Rajneesh, the city council transferred the deed back to the Episcopal Diocese of Eastern Oregon. As soon as the Rajneeshees were in charge, they said the church should be making money for the town. That statement, coupled with the rumor that a professional gambler from Nevada was going to move to Antelope, caused local folks to add two and two and find a church in jeopardy.

If you want to see listlessness, usual apathy and indifference quickly turn into an assertive, whirring buzz, just tell folks who were christened, wed and otherwise blessed in a little, white country church that it is about to be used as an economical adjunct for a philosopher whose writings embrace the destruction of the family unit and propose unfettered sex as the most direct route to spiritual enlightenment.

In June of 1983, the determined Rajneeshee city council sued the Episcopalian Diocese for the return of the deed and asked for $5.00 a day from May 24, 1982. They also sued the old city council, Margaret Hill, Phil Hill, Al Kuhlman, Betty Anderson, Frances Dickson and Don Smith, requesting damages of not less that $10,000, due to their "illegal" actions.

The diocese attorney, James R. Foster, said a trust had been created, and the actions of the city and school board were consistent with maintaining the trust. He further said that the trust would have been broken if the deed had not been returned.

The Right Reverend Rustin R. Kimsey, Bishop of the Episcopal Diocese of Eastern Oregon, said the diocese was, "very intent on defending the property for the use of the Christian community."

Ma Prem Sangeet said, "The purpose of the defendants was to keep control of the church in the hands of Protestant Christians. That is a violation of the First Amendment." (They entered every battle holding up the First amendment as a shield.)

The Sunday following Judge Copenhaver's decision, in favor of the diocese, the church attendance swelled to 97 with all voices joined in prayerful, melodious thanks with "How Great Thou Art."

The first indication that the school building, and its monthly operating check, was coveted by the Rajneeshees was at the school board meeting of February 22, 1982, when Dave

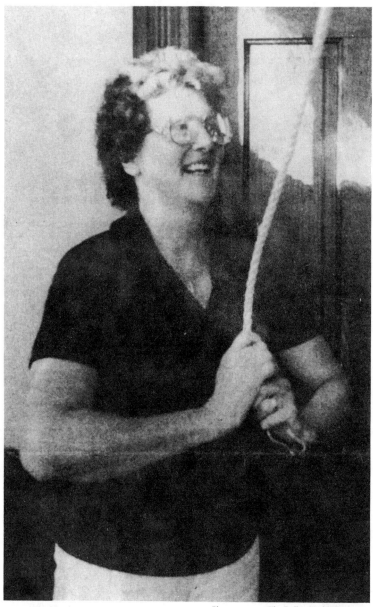

Photo courtesy *The Dalles Weekly Reminder*

Frances Dickson triumphantly rings the community church bell.

Antelope Community Church

Antelope School

Knapp (City Slick, again) said that Rajneeshees should fill the two board vacancies, in order to avoid "taxation without representation."

Rancher Frank McNamee stated that some of the large taxpaying ranches had not been represented for as long as forty years, and those owners did not feel the necessity to sit on the board. The state of Oregon offered them their own school district on their ranch, but Dave Knapp said the state would require "too much paper work."

The northern part of Rancho Rajneesh was in the Antelope school district—number 50J, and thus they had the voting power to control budget levies. After they twice voted down operating funds, schoolboard chairman Dareld McCall reluctantly announced that school was out—permanently—after ninety years of service to the community.

With the school closed and children to be educated, the district, encompassing some two hundred square miles, had to be divided between Madras and Maupin. About fifty property owners petitioned to be annexed to Madras, even though it would mean a bus ride over eighty miles roundtrip for some students, including kindergarten children. Madras agreed to the merger, but it could not take affect until May 31, 1984.

Those folks who had been paying into the Antelope district now found that tuition was required by Madras to cover expenses until May 1984, and then it was that the Rajneeshees agreed to vote for a levy in the amount of $25,000. In return for their affirmative votes, they said they would open the Antelope school.

Dareld McCall said of their plan, "They will approve the levy, at a cost to them of $12,000, and in return, they will get nearly $60,000 next August from the state. They'll come out way ahead."

But on election day, in true Rajneesh fashion, Rajneeshees defeated the levy 429 to 45. Then they opened the school. Schoolboard chairman Swami Wadud welcomed non-Rajneesh children, but parents were adamant—their children would not attend classes with Rajneeshees nor would they be taught by Rajneeshee teachers.

The state attorney general, David Frohnmayer, said their teachers could not wear religious garb, and he asked state school superintendent Verne Duncan to hold up the October operating check of $2,236.00 until a fact-finding team could determine whether or not their school complied with state standards.

Verne Duncan sent a five-person committee which found that the district lacked the curriculum and sufficient certified teachers: however, they were addressing these short-comings. Duncan said that since it was a legally constituted public school district, he had to release the funds, and he did.

The Rajneeshees operated the school with an attendance from 50 to 120 students, encompassing kindergarten through high school. Each year their projected budget rose, until in the fiscal year of 1986-87 it was $106,000.

On March 15, 1985 Vern Duncan again withheld state support funds. The Rajneeshees had moved grades four through high school to Rajneeshpuram where only 2 hours a day in a classroom were required, and the remainder of the day was spent working on Rajneeshee projects for which the children were given academic credit. Duncan said it was against state law for the school to aid a religious organization.

On March 20 the district sued the state seeking to force the restoration of state financing. They assured the state that their "school without doors" program, as they called it, had been abandoned. This time state officials visited the school to ascertain the truth. Funds were released on March 29. From October 1983 through March of 1986, they collected state funds in the amount of $107,575.00 and this was in addition to county funds.

FOURTEEN

The immigration office is under the jurisdiction of the Department of Justice. The head of this department told Janet and me in 1983 that Bhagwan would be deported by 1985. "But we don't have that long!" Janet told him in frustration.

And so we kept up our vigil at the local immigration office, always hoping to hear the good news. It was in the winter of 1984 when we last stopped in for a briefing. An investigator, with whom we were well-acquainted, was in the hall at the water fountain. When he saw us, without straightening up, he looked furtively up and down the halls and whispered, "Can't tell you anything today." We left feeling as if we had just been a part of a cloak and dagger mystery.

Those of us who were closely following the federal investigation knew criminal indictments were imminent, and that news leaked out to Bhagwan. He waited just long enough for Sheela to depart for Germany, and then he took to the airwaves and cast all the blame for criminal acts on her and her cohorts. It was easy for the citizens of Oregon to believe him; after all, hadn't we observed her venomous attacks, found her actions contrary to her words and heard her ruthlessly rail against public officials?

We had seen her play many roles, and many of these we will forget—such as when she kissed the Bhagwan's feet as she prostrated herself before him on the pavement in front of the local immigration office; and when she gave the opening prayer at the state legislature—with head and arms lifted upward, she gave a Hindi chant; and when she placed a wreath at the grave of Oregon's great statesman, Governor Tom McCall. We will forget these.

But she will be well-remembered from Washington D.C. to the Antelope Valley for her rapier-sharp tongue, which on two occasions pronounced me "That ugly redheaded b___."

She was a true dichotomy. She exercised her right to

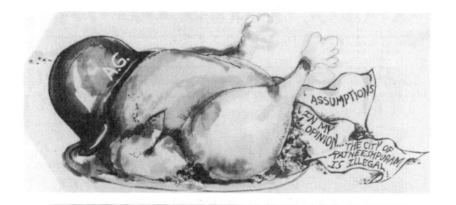

The Frohnmayer "Best Buy"

Our vote for this year's Top Turkey must go to the "Herr General" breed, raised exclusively on Oregon's protein-enriched "bigots barley" and stuffed with 49-55 pages of opinions and assumptions on the separation of church and state.

The Rajneesh Times was laced with satirical criticisms and unkind caricatures of their foes. This Thanksgiving turkey is a sample of their barbed wit levelled at the attorney general—a favorite subject.

These clippings of Ma Anand Sheela typify her arrogance.

"At this point the Attorney General should resign and declare himself illegal."

speak beyond the limits of decency, and at the same time, under the tutelage of Bhagwan, she deprived followers of *their* rights. Many of them will remember her as the wicked stepmother from the East.

In an attempt to recoup some of his investment in Antelope, before he too would depart, he offered to sell back properties to the oldtime residents, who by now were well-established elsewhere. No one wanted to return to Antelope, where his intimidating police force was still present, plus, the highest city tax base in the state.

Bhagwan quickly left for Bermuda, but when his plane made a fuel stop in Charleston, North Carolina, federal officials arrested him and seven of his trusted followers. They impounded his throne, a suitcase full of diamond-studded jewelry, and fifty-five thousand dollars in cash. He insisted he was not departing the states—only leaving for a short, restful vacation arranged by his followers!

Twelve days later he was back in Oregon in jail. He pleaded guilty to only two of the thirty-six counts against him and promised to leave the country. (His wish in the first place.) His plea-bargaining was successful, and so eager was he to leave that within five hours he was gone. His only penalty was the payment of a fine in the amount of four hundred thousand dollars and a promise not to return for five years. (Why five years? Why not forever?) Even though it would have cost thousand of dollars, I believe he should have been taken, step by step, through the legal system and given the maximum punishment for his crimes. I do not believe in plea bargaining.

For six months he traveled the world seeking a new homesite. He was rejected or ejected from every country in which he sought refuge. The Greeks in Crete threatened him with fatal stoning because of his immoral teachings. Rumors circulated that he was going to live in the Fiji Islands, but before he could disembark, he was advised to stay away. In June of 1986 he entered Uruguay, but the day after he announced that he was going to build a commune, he was asked to leave

144 THE RAJNEESH STORY

as soon as possible.

He next went to Jamaica. His stay was short. Because of "his unattractive reputation," he was asked to leave. The videotape of his testimony for my trial was not needed in order to inform the world of his wicked ways. He was exposed by his inability to conform to acceptable social behavior and his obdurate belief that there is no law in any land that binds him. After a total of twenty-one countries refused him entry, he was forced to return to India. Stringent restrictions were placed upon his activities there.

From New Delhi he was seen on worldwide television telling the audience that the United States was a hell of a place to live. From New Delhi he traveled northeast into the garden spot of the East where he finally ran out of paved roads.

In the spring of 1985 Sheela went to Nepal across the border from northeast India, and some of us speculated then that she sought a new place for Bhagwan and the hierarchy, but Nepal has no roads. The only transportation is upon the backs of elephants. If Bhagwan had stayed in Nepal, he would have had roads built with the same ease with which he so quickly built a complete city in the sagebrush—a city complete with a shopping mall, hotel, city hall, airport and crematorium. (The state of Oregon licensed one of their physicians as a coroner.) Pervasive, macabre thoughts filled my heart and soul anytime their crematorium was mentioned.

Although they used it at other times, it seemed as if each year at the peak of their summer celebrations, it became necessary to use the samadhi, and always between 7,000 and 10,000 sang and danced in the lecture hall (two football fields in size) to help send the deceased on to their greatest enlightenment.

Swami Dhyan Nirvesh, a.k.a. Thomas Utne, died from acute asthma, and 8,000 celebrants helped him to a "magnificent send-off," according to Ma Ananda Sarita.

Swami Adinatha, from Tokyo, drowned in their man-made lake, and Sheela said, "Let us thank Swami Adinatha for giving us an opportunity to celebrate." Ten thousand helped in his transition.

The bodies were always covered with flowers before being placed on a pyre which was fired with juniper wood and propane. The area was enclosed in glass to prevent sparks, and a large chimney carried the juniper-incense upward. It took about four hours to turn "ashes to ashes."

As the news reached us of these cremations, at the height of their money-making celebrations, I could not help but think that those who took part in these activities paid to do so.

When it became known that the fall of the empire on the Old Muddy ranch was just a matter of time, and Sheela was in Germany, and the Bhagwan accused her of all the nefarious deeds, they fired a body again.

A news report from Rajneeshpuram claimed that two sannyasins had AIDS and were kept in isolation to protect other sannyasins. I immediately called Janet and told her I believed those two were healthy members of the hierarchy who, with the turmoil and jockeying for power, were too glib of tongue—probably wanted to put some facts straight, and that was why they were being kept incommunicado. She agreed, but it was only conjecture on our part.

Within a few days another Rajneeshpuram news release stated that one of these AIDS victims had been cremated. (More macabre thoughts with which to deal.) I called Gertrude Thompson, the governor's chief aide, and said to her, "It's my opinion, they are killing people over there." She said, "Yes, Donna. We are looking into that right now."

In January of 1990 word from Poona was that the Bhagwan was dead and had been cremated. His epitaph was. "Never born, never died, visited the planet Earth between Dec. 11, 1931 and Jan. 19, 1990."

I could fantasize that a follower was his proxy on the funeral pyre, and that he now roams the world a welcome, wealthy traveler, sans beard and ceremonial robes; however, he was nurtured, fed and reveled in publicity. Anonymity was not for Bhagwan!

And so he died without spending the millions purported to be his. What happened to the forty-three million dollars in a Swiss bank account and the money in his business office in London? What happened to the money from the Texas auto dealer who bought his eight-seven Rolls Royces? And the money from the sale of the Muddy ranch—what happened to that? Wasco county collected $1.5 million dollars from that sale for back taxes. The actual selling price was not disclosed by the purchaser—a multimillionaire, Dennis Washington, from Montana.

Worth noting here is a pertinent comment on communes written by Don Roberts of the Hillsboro Argus (Hillsboro, Oregon) "The communal living philosophy is completely foreign to the Judeo-Christian ethic and the free enterprise and property right systems which form the background of this nation. What is called for is broad public education stressing what is right with American ideals and what is wrong with popular cults which rob individuals both of their God given rights and their intrinsic powers of reason."

Bhagwan had his own perverted concept of communal living as noted in The Sound of Running Water. "My concept is that of a commune, not of a family. Families have to disappear, communes should exist. Prostitution is a by-product of marriage, and unless marriage disappears, prostitution is going to remain."

With the fall of the commune, the Rajneeshee government in Antelope disintegrated with a mass resignation. Wasco County had to appoint local residents to the seven vacancies. In 1981, with thirty-nine residents, it was an impossible task to elect seven community-spirited residents and not include those with self-serving aspirations. A sign in the post office window urged residents to volunteer; however, few are inclined to enter a fray that pits neighbor against neighbor.

And so it was with the Rajneeshee school officials. With the deportation of the Bhagwan, they resigned en masse. When Wasco county advertised for new schoolboard members, no one responded. Students and teachers quickly diminished. School terminated in the summer of 1986—this time forever, but the building still serves as a gathering place for community functions. The harvest dinner at Thanksgiving time—an event favored by all—continues to remind the valley residents there is yet much for which to be thankful.

Sheela Silverman was extradited from Germany, and on July 22, 1986, she pleaded guilty to the salmonella poisoning of seven hundred and fifty residents of The Dalles. The culture was grown in their underground laboratory at Rajneeshpuram, where they also were experimenting with the AIDS virus. Three salad bars in The Dalles were contaminated with the salmonella in what was the largest mass-poisoning attempt in the United States. Did they intend to eliminate county voters with this extreme method?

She also admitted to illegal wiretapping, the attempted murder of the Bhagwan's doctor and the attempted poisoning of two of the Wasco county commissioners. The three commissioners had visited Rajneeshpuram in hot August of 1984, asked for a drink of water and two of them, Hulse and Matthew, were poisoned. Judge Hulse became dangerously ill, but survived, and the "sleepy-eyed" one escaped, because they found in him no foe to their goals.

Sheela was meted two terms of four and one-half years to be served concurrently in a minimum security penitentiary in Pleasanton, California. She served twenty-nine months and was deported to Germany.

City Slick, a.k.a. David Berry Knapp, was given two years in a federal jail over the objections of his defense attorney who felt he deserved freedom, because he had turned state's evidence. Even the prosecuting United States attorney requested he be given probation, but presiding Judge Edward Leavy ruled that he be incarcerated. Antelopeans praised his decision; after all City Slick was the ever-present antagonist of the old-timers who found his behavior unconscionable.

The sagebrush empire began to crumble into desert dust, when Bhagwan ordered hundreds of sham marriages between his foreign followers and citizens of the United States. The Department of Justice, through the immigration authorities, jerked the foundation out from under his edifice, and it was no more.

Sitting in positions of power in Oregon, both in public and private service, are those who gave aid to Rajneesh. Now they must live their lives atoning through their conscience.

Conclusion

The Bhagwan's doves have come down, and the likeness of the graceful antelope has gone up on the sign in front of the eight-stool cafe, where the locals, new and old, gather once again to discuss the important and mundane and enjoy a difference of opinion.

The major dispute, which began in 1986, was whether to disincorporate or not, and the minor argument was whether to permit chickens within the town's boundaries.

There is always much to ponder when living in that small hamlet, where residents are so few they look upon one another as family when one is in need, and like family, they state opposing opinions with gusto, but in the fall they all sit down together for a harvest dinner, and at Christmas their voices are joined in song.

Antelopeans are scrappy, but the American traditions and precepts upon which this country was founded are in practice daily such as the strong handclasp so freely given to express camaraderie, to greet a friend, to welcome a stranger and to bind a contract. Antelopeans live exemplary lives— honorable life-styles elicited as much by the prevalent gossips as the Ten Commandments.

Their Main street is not a direct route to any place, but there will always be those sojourners who will deliberately find the town and stop at the cafe, as I did in 1970. They will find different folks there, who, after a questioning glance, will make them feel at home. That is just the way it is in Antelope. And should a stranger encounter one of the famous forty residents, who knows firsthand of the onslaught, it would be wise not to probe that subject, because the veterans of that red war, like veterans of any war, bear scars. Recovery has been slow. For some, recovery is not possible.

The valley remains the same, though some of its inhabitants have changed. It's pristine beauty, the mournful cry of the dove, the early morning visits of browsing deer, and the

call of the meadowlark have beckoned to other doggedly determined, indomitable folks who now fill the houses emptied
by the guru's followers.

Just as the hardy strain of the desert wheat emerges each
spring to grow strong against the summer's wind, bending but
not breaking before its enemy, enduring until its golden harvest, so it is with the hardy strain of folks who choose to live
there, each nurturing a spirit imbued with the faith that the
natural progression of life corrects all its ills.

THE END

ABOUT THE AUTHOR

Donna Quick was born and reared in Portland, Oregon. Family vacations were spent on the Greiger dairy farm on the Lewis River near Woodland, Washington, where she developed a deep appreciation of nature and her critters. For 25 years she raised fine quarterhorses and kept several pet cows on a mini-farm in northwest Portland.

She is a successful artist in oils and a knowledgeable collector of objects from the past. With nostalgia as her subject, she has written for The Oregonian and the paper's former Sunday magazine Northwest and, extensively, for the Hillsboro Argus.

Her hobby of driving the backroads of Oregon took her to Antelope, where she purchased and then laboriously returned an 1897 cottage to its original country charm.

It is there that this story begins.